GOING ALL IN

HOW TO IMPLEMENT EXCELLENCE IN YOUR BUSINESS

Mark Rehn and Mark James

ISBN: 978-0-6487369-1-2

Contact Details

My Business Excellence®

Web: mybusinessexcellence.com

Phone: 1300 722 815

Email: hello@mybusinessexcellence.com

For Helen and Kim, with love and many thanks for your forbearance and support over the years

Contents

FOREWORD

For the past decade I have coached and mentored hundreds of CEOs, business owners and key executives who are members of the international TEC and Vistage networks. In addition, I have spent 20 years in CEO and senior executive positions at national and international, manufacturing and marketing companies.

During my career I've found that the growth of most SMEs (10-500 employees) can plateau at times. Owners and managers of these organizations may then struggle to either regain momentum or build traction in a constantly changing business landscape.

To avoid that happening, the organization needs a well-founded strategic plan followed by a successful implementation. It is in these areas most SMEs fail and so do not achieve their potential.

Even if a clear strategy is identified, one that gives them a competitive advantage, it is often not realized. Every business strives to have that unique product or service, but most don't achieve that differentiation in practice. Complexity is often seen as the way to get it when in fact simplicity would be the differentiator. Actually, delivering the business promises of the strategy in the most efficient way would make them significantly 'different and better' and yield the competitive advantage they seek.

The My Business Excellence (MBE) approach provides the framework and proven techniques to achieve this competitive advantage.

It can be delivered by the MBE team coaching your organization through their approach, and now you have direct access to all the practical details of that approach with this marvelous book. It provides a complete roadmap for you to institute the MBE approach and ensure you remain on this guaranteed path to success.

Harvey Martin, TEC Master Coach and Mentor to CEOs, Managing Directors, Business Owners, Senior Executives and Peer Advisory Boards.

INTRODUCTION

"If you always do what you've always done, you'll always get what you've always got."

Henry Ford (1863-1947)

Imagine you're standing at the top of a cliff, peering down a few hundred feet to the rocky shore below. Imagine a fire behind you, slowly burning its way towards the cliff edge. Now imagine there's a ship out to sea, on the horizon. It can't get to you, but if you can reach it, you'll be able to sail away. You're trapped between the proverbial rock and a hard place, with a choice to make. You can step forward into the unknown and fall to your death. Or you can stay put, refuse to change, and be asphyxiated.

Change often feels like that. You know you can't stay where you are, but you're paralyzed with fear about what the future holds; all the things that can go wrong, and the uncertainty of it all. You can see the future you want, but you don't know how to get there. You know if you don't take charge and initiate change yourself, eventually you will be overtaken and left behind, but you don't know how to make the change you want to see happen.

In business, the fire behind you is all too real. It's the tide of change and progress. While Henry Ford may have been right about repeating the same process producing the same results, what he didn't mention is that over time those results will diminish. The cliff edge of the future and the rocks below are all too ready to consume a failing business that resists change, or one that enforces change blindly in a panic to put out the fire.

Now imagine you're on that same cliff edge, with the same fire burning behind you, and the same ship out to sea, but you are strapped into a hang glider. You know all you have to do is take a run up and jump, and the frame above you will keep you in the air. Either you'll glide gently to a safe distance, and reach the boat, or you'll soar and fly. Either way, you won't crash on the rocks or be consumed by the flames. Do you think you might take that step forward?

The ship out to sea is your future business, where all your processes are aligned with your core values and goals. It's the ship that runs smoothly, with every employee working on the business as well as in it, and where change is a normal part of business. The hang glider? The My Business Excellence® (MBE) approach that will get you off that cliff without leaving you to either crash or burn.

Unlike other change and process management approaches, MBE is designed to work for companies with as few as 10 employees, and to scale up as the business grows with up to 500 employees. It's not designed for larger businesses. And it's not couched in corporate speak. It's designed to be simple; easy to remember and to implement.

By implementing the MBE approach with simple, integrated and sequential steps, any SME can pursue excellence in an efficient, low cost manner. Better yet, because the system is designed to deal with the low-hanging fruit first, businesses realize substantial net benefits well within the first year of their journey.

Is the MBE Approach for You?

So, who is the MBE approach for? And who should read this book?

The MBE approach is for Small to Medium Enterprises (SMEs). We adopt the European definition of SME[1] expanded a little, i.e., those with 10-49 full-time employees (Small Enterprise) and those with 50-250 or more (up to 500) full-time employees (Medium Enterprise). This book is aimed primarily at the CEOs and Owners of those companies who are ambitious and keen on business growth. In addition, members of SME Management Teams and others who may aspire to becoming a CEO will find the book particularly relevant.

To be clear, the MBE approach will work for even very small businesses with only 10 full-time employees. Although we specify certain key roles, this doesn't mean you need separate people to fulfil each of those roles. In a very small business, these part-time roles may be shared by the employees that currently report direct to the CEO.

Similarly, although for larger SMEs we recommend running multiple projects simultaneously, a very small business might start with a single project and build up from there. To comply with the approach and extract the maximum possible benefits, all you need is one or more autonomous teams of 3 or 4 people doing local projects at the bottom of the organization every quarter. The trick is to target the right projects. Overall, implementing the MBE approach is a combined top-down, bottom-up process.

The MBE approach is designed primarily for service-based businesses. If you are involved in manufacturing, you will likely already be using somewhat similar and overlapping tools. That's not to say MBE can't add value to manufacturing businesses. After all, every manufacturing business has a service dimension. We have had many clients in manufacturing who have benefited greatly from the approach. But mostly we work with "white collar" businesses such as accountancies, legal firms, engineering consultants, construction firms or other service-type businesses with high labor costs and delivering high business value, but where formal process improvements are still lacking.

Please note that the MBE approach is not aimed at business startups. To get the most out of the approach, you need to have a functioning business model. Marketing and selling of your offerings should already be underway.

An important principle is that all business, whether in the manufacturing or service sectors, is done through processes. Process design and improvement therefore features as the core aspect of the MBE approach. We recommend a particularly simple but powerful methodology for this—far simpler than the Six Sigma methodology[2] so often adopted by manufacturing businesses. We believe applying Six Sigma in a service-oriented SME is akin to using a sledgehammer to crack a nut.

Why listen to us?

Let's cut to the heart of the matter up front. Why should you listen to us? Why should you commit your time and that of your employees to implementing the MBE approach, and not some other business improvement philosophy?

We're teaching and doing this every day. It's who we are. It's what we live and breathe.

Dr Mark Rehn, (a.k.a. The Old Guy) has been in the business improvement game for nearly forty years. In the 1980s, he led the teams that developed the World Competitive Manufacturing (WCM) and Total Quality Management (TQM) methodologies for Australia and New Zealand. He introduced them into Australian and New Zealand SMEs via several hundred specially trained consultancy firms[3]. His co-owned consulting firm, Aptech Australia, worked almost exclusively with SMEs for 15 years. He subsequently undertook leadership roles in Business Transformation, Strategic Partnering, and Knowledge Management for IBM Global Services in Australia, New Zealand and the Asia Pacific Region.

Since leaving IBM in 2001, Dr Rehn has helped his SME clients understand and implement business excellence as an independent consultant. He has progressively converted his successful consulting methodology into the My Business Excellence® web-based offering exclusively for SMEs.

Mark James (a.k.a. The Young Guy) comes from an Information Technology (IT) background. He has been consulting in data analytics, custom software systems and technology strategy for businesses in Australia, Europe and Asia for years—across a wide range of SMEs and Enterprises as a consultant and then for his own business. Through these engagements, he came to realize that the difference between successful software implementations and those that disappointed came down to whether the business understood that software *enables* process rather than defines it. Recognizing the importance of process thinking and that successful software implementations always require a strategic perspective, he adopted parts of the MBE approach to complement his own techniques. Mark James is now our CEO.

Every few weeks, we give a presentation to 15 or so CEOs from SMEs who are keen to improve their business performance. The feedback we receive is they like what we do because it gives them a simple structure and a kick-start to genuine business transformation at low cost. It works because we use simple language and simple, proven techniques.

We also take a holistic approach to business excellence. We don't focus on managing finances, or personnel, or any other specific sub-set of business management. We start with the overall picture, and we focus on helping our clients become world class at what they are doing in all areas of the business.

Three years ago, we sat down to discuss our own business methodology. We wanted to be able to scale up access to the MBE approach without having to employ and manage hundreds of consultants and facilitators. We also wanted to go global. The problem, of course, is that we both live and work in Australia. While we're happy to travel to help clients implement the approach, that would limit our ability to reach more businesses. And the attendant costs involved in helping lots of overseas clients via face-to-face consulting would be substantial.

Instead, we wanted to develop a way for CEOs and their Management Teams to implement the approach themselves; a Do-It-Yourself (DIY) option. We were convinced that with access to the right guidance, software, tools and techniques, they would be able to understand and apply the whole system from end to end without our direct consulting input.

This book acts as a practical 'how to' guide. It introduces all the important concepts and provides practical examples for how you can implement excellence the way we do for our clients.

While this book alone is enough for you to implement excellence in your business, we want to make sure you can access more help if and when you need it. Appendix A provides further resources that will help you implement the critical steps of this approach. Make sure you review Appendix A once you decide that the MBE approach is right for you and your business.

What's in the book?

Too many books on business management either take a thought leadership approach and lay out the philosophy of a specific approach, but are thin on the how-to details. Or else they take a clinical, management style approach to "how-to" for a particular partial solution to the overall problem, and leave readers asleep at the wheel.

Our overall aim in publishing this book is to give you a balanced blend of the philosophical, methodical, and practical so that you can confidently embark on your journey towards excellence.

Armed with our detailed guidance, you will be in charge of the implementation, not some external consultant charging big dollars.

In PART 1: Why My Business Excellence®? you will learn why you ought to do this and the mindset you will need to see it through.

In PART 2: What Is My Business Excellence®? you will see what you're going to do at a high level. You will be introduced to the main elements of the approach, and how they all fit together.

In PART 3: Implementing My Business Excellence® you will learn the roles, tools, and timelines you'll need to apply the approach in practice.

After reading this book, you will be faced with two options:

1. **Do nothing**. Put this book down, forget about its contents and carry on as you were before, working in your business instead of on it. Hopefully, you will understand why this is the least beneficial option: You won't improve your business, you won't solve the problem that made you pick up the book, and you will suffer the costs of lost opportunity as your business continues to stagnate in the critical areas of process management, strategy deployment, performance measurement, knowledge management, and change leadership and management.

2. **Implement the approach outlined in this book** and become a world class organization in your industry, gaining the recognition, growth and profitability you desire along the way.

"One of the best business decisions we have made, it has enabled our company to achieve significant improvements across a range of different areas. My Business Excellence® has far exceeded our expectations and very quickly paid for our investment."

Craig Musson, Managing Director, WAFEX

PART 1:

WHY MY BUSINESS EXCELLENCE®?

A Little History

About 40 years ago, Dr. Mark Rehn co-founded a management consulting business called Aptech Australia and focused on introducing business excellence into SMEs. Why business excellence? Because there seemed to be no shortage of gurus preaching the gospel about their own favored subset of skills and achieving excellence in specific areas, but no one seemed to be addressing the big picture of holistic change in a very practical way. Every business is a complete system and needs to be treated as such when introducing transformational change. If not, change introduced into one part of the system will have significant adverse impacts on other parts of the system.

Aptech Australia therefore developed a systemic change methodology, jokingly referred to in those days as "The Seven Steps to Heaven". (Those seven steps were very similar to the current Prerequisites of our MBE Reference Framework). Aptech started providing consulting advice in the context of this "big picture", with emphasis on the business need for sound strategy development and its deployment by means of the organization's agreed Key Processes. The twin ideas of having all the Key Processes depicted on one page, and all the strategic Objectives also depicted on one page date as far back as 1982.

Dr Rehn explains that he was doing the rounds as a guest speaker on the national and international circuits, advocating this simple approach for business excellence thinking and its implementation:

> *"The more I did those sessions, the more I was convinced we were on the right track to talk about putting it all together with a key emphasis on pragmatism. A lot of consulting offerings we saw around the world were designed to retain intellectual property and only progressively reveal it when the consultants were engaged. We just felt that was the wrong way to go about it. So, ever since we have been open with respect to the approach."*

Dr Rehn estimates that he has personally spoken to over 3,000 CEOs of SMEs over the last 35 years. After a long career in the field, Dr Rehn is looking to wind down his personal involvement in the direct consulting practice, and at the same time help scale up the MBE approach for an international audience.

In 2012, he engaged Mark James and his company to explore how software could be used to assist implementation of the ever-evolving MBE approach. Mark James has since become increasingly involved in the development of both the approach and the *associated software*. The original contracted relationship with Dr Rehn has evolved into a close working relationship. Mark James became CEO in 2018.

While Dr Rehn continues to conduct awareness workshops and in-house speaking engagements for CEOs and Management Teams, Mark James has taken over from Dr Rehn as the lead consultant for the MBE approach. He became the CEO in December 2018. He is also available for awareness workshops and speaking engagements.

What It Means to Become Excellent

As the CEO of an SME, you're already spending a large amount of time trying to improve your business. Long hours spent writing goals and Objectives, setting timelines, educating management and employees, and prioritizing your endless list of daily, weekly, and monthly obligations only seem to keep you running on the treadmill but effectively staying in the same place.

We've seen this a thousand times and we understand how frustrating this can be. It's like you're a racehorse pulling a plough; meant for greater things but stuck in the muddy potato field.

You need to ask yourself:

- With all your effort and heroic endurance, why aren't things any different?
- Why are some other businesses steadily achieving their goals and meeting their financial benchmarks when you have been struggling so long and so hard?
- What is the difference between your business and a high-performing business, one that is regarded as excellent and highly successful?

It's in your approach.

It's not always what you do, but the way you do it. Let's say that again. The WAY you introduce your improvement initiatives is the key difference between success and continuing struggles through the mud of inertia.

Most SMEs make improvements reactively, rather than being carefully planned and coordinated. The necessary vision, protocols, management, and assessments are either lacking or not being tracked. These ad hoc improvements usually falter and fade away over time because they have not been properly introduced, reinforced, and standardized.

Figure 1 illustrates this state of affairs:

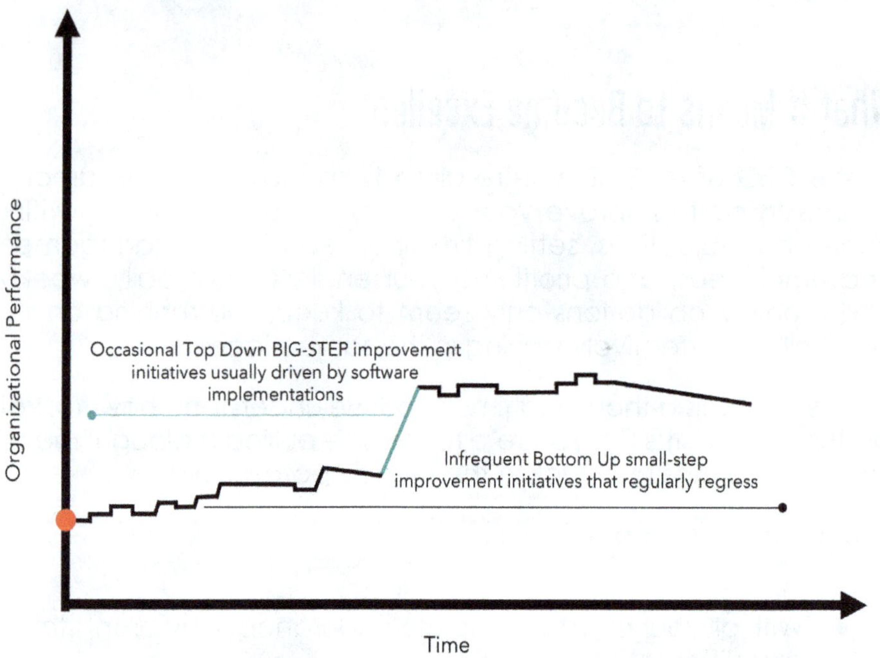

Figure 1: Typical performance profile for an SME

To build and maintain a high performing business, you need to implement improvements based on a management system that supports the changes and maximizes their effectiveness. Once implementing change is accepted by all as the new way of doing things, the compounding effects of steady and permanent improvements result in high performance.

Figure 2 illustrates the dramatic impact.

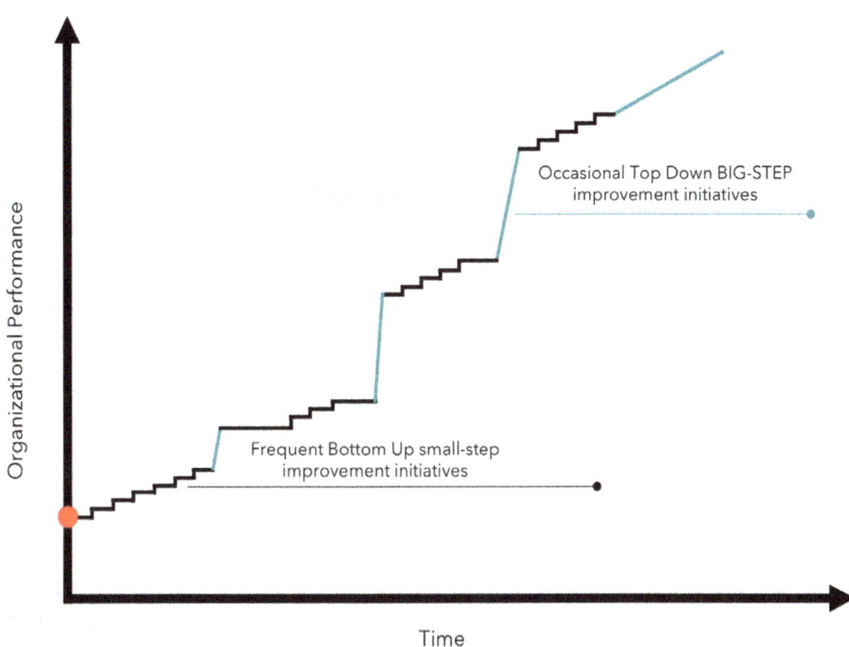

Figure 2: High performance profile for an SME

You may have canvassed the variety of solutions available in the marketplace that promise to improve some aspect of your business. But the truth is that improvements focusing on one aspect of business are only partial solutions. Implemented in isolation, they do not help a business in the long run. In fact, they prevent it from ever reaching its full potential. For instance, it's no good having an excellent sales process but a shoddy product. Or an excellent product with a poor customer experience due to chaotic logistics and indifferent customer support.

To become a high-performing business excelling at the highest level, only an integrated, comprehensive system for change—tailored to the specific needs of your company—will achieve maximum profitability and deliver the personal satisfaction you crave.

This book shows how you can orchestrate the comprehensive and long-lasting improvement of your SME as quickly and effectively as possible—and at the lowest possible cost.

But before we go any further, let's define some key words and concepts.

Business Excellence

When we talk about business excellence, we mean across-the-board performance. Excellence must extend to all areas of the business system for maximum impact.

In order for your business to achieve excellence across the board and reach its full potential, the business must become excellent at business improvement. You need to focus on processes you are trying to change as well as on the process of change management. Makes sense, right?

Perhaps you have come across the Japanese term *kaizen*. Roughly translated, kaizen means never-ending improvement towards perfection. While perfection will never be achieved, continually improving processes and associated support systems will lead to ever-increasing levels of success.

But improving processes alone is not enough. In today's rapidly changing business environment, you also need to have a dynamic and flexible approach to the deployment of strategy.

Business Excellence thus consists of two big and interlinked components—Operational excellence and Strategic excellence.

Operational Excellence

Operational excellence focuses on all the processes needed to RUN your business.

Our feedback from CEOs suggests that about 90% of SMEs don't have well defined and documented processes that ensure smooth and efficient running. Instead, they have informal or ad hoc processes that have evolved over time, and often end up compromising the effectiveness of each other. Improvements made to these processes typically end up being temporary, malformed, and inconsistent. This is the opposite of what you want.

Here is an example. We recently worked with an electrical engineering firm. Whenever a drawing or a specification changed during an engineering project, they were required to send a transmittal which indicated to all the stakeholders what's been changed and why. But they had no standard way of doing it. Some people were sending the transmittals and others weren't. This wasn't just a matter of poor practice. It also constituted a huge liability risk. This simple process failure could easily have cost them big dollars if, months later, something wasn't done that should have been, or machinery had been built to an out-of-date specification.

They recognized the need for urgent improvement to this operational process. We facilitated a fast process improvement project for them and found the following root causes:

1. **No formal agreement on triggering criteria.** Without clear guidance on when to send a transmittal and when not to, people were relying on their best judgement, which was inconsistent.

2. **No formal template for a transmittal.** Without clear guidance on what to include, people sent the information they thought was necessary, and this too was inconsistent.

3. **Too time consuming.** With no template and no consistent approach, transmittals took too long to compile with no prospect of automating any of the steps (because they weren't defined!). So, when they got busy, they tended to skip sending a transmittal.

Having identified the top three root causes of the problem, the improvement team quickly agreed on the triggering criteria for sending a transmittal. They then created a transmittal template and communicated the new approach to staff and appropriate stakeholders.

The directors are now relieved, knowing they are no longer sitting on a ticking time bomb for liability. Employees have clear guidelines and expectations, and stakeholders have increased confidence in the company's professionalism and ability to manage and deliver projects.

Sadly, feedback from CEOs we talk to suggests only around 5% of SMEs are routinely applying best practice techniques that result in permanent process improvements for their operational processes. This is the foundation for business success and yet the vast majority are missing out on the benefits. Is your business one of those?

Operational excellence deals with the way you and your people work IN your business. Excessive wait times, working at cross-purposes between departments, and duplication of effort are just three of the many barriers to Operational excellence.

Case Study: Australian Securities and Investments Commission (ASIC) – Pervasive application of process improvement projects in the public sector

Operational excellence is a term usually associated with private sector organizations focused on generating customer delight by driving improvements in how they deliver products and services. It is founded on a commitment to continuous improvement in how processes affect users inside and outside the enterprise.

While the benefits of Operational excellence have been long established in the business world, there is now a growing trend for the public sector to take advantage of this process-centric approach.

Most public sector agencies today understand their responsibility for external and internal customers and are looking for ways to speed processes and cut costs. There are a number of drivers for this, including:

- Tight budgets
- An aging worker population
- Data security
- Customer complaints
- Cross-governmental pressures for interoperability and information sharing
- New information and communication technologies
- Legislative and regulatory compliance
- Need to better integrate siloed functions and systems, reducing the hand-offs between them
- Continuity of operations

Since 2012, ASIC has improved its operations by adopting the MBE approach for occasional top-down Business Process Reengineering (BPR) Projects and frequent bottom-up Fast Process Improvement (FPI) projects. ASIC's main focus to date has been on a continuous stream of large BPR projects aimed at maximizing the use and benefits of new IT systems for each of their many Case types that need to be managed.

The Benefits realized by ASIC:

- Online, end-to-end Case Management System
- Faster information access and delivery
- Information available to all users at all locations
- Operational "silos" largely eliminated
- Reduced operational costs

From the outset, ASIC chose not to adopt the MBE approach for developing and implementing strategy. Most, but not all, of our other public sector clients have done likewise. Faced with frequent leadership changes, short-term governmental pressures and the need to comply with a complex array of rules and regulations, Operational excellence tends to be the main concern of public sector organizations rather than Strategic excellence.

Strategic Excellence

Strategic Excellence focuses on the best ways to CHANGE your business.

Strategic excellence comes from the quality of thought about why you do what you do, and about what you should do differently.

When process improvements driven by your strategic Objectives are initiated and managed properly, the quality of products and services increases, and your customers become more satisfied with the value of their purchases. Big financial benefits result. Your employees also benefit from having a better work-life balance.

Strategic excellence starts with having a clear and shared strategic plan. But it doesn't stop there. The strategic plan must be executed, preferably in full. Sadly, it is widely reported (e.g., by the American Management Association[4]) that some 60% of strategic plans fail to get executed properly.

And here are two additional sobering statistics about strategy execution from a recent Dutch survey[4]:

1. Only 50% of leaders rated implementation as equal in importance to strategy formulation.

2. Only 2% of leaders are confident they will achieve 80-100% of their strategy's Objectives.

Strategic excellence is not an alternative to Operational excellence, but rather is complementary and enhancing. The best thought in the world won't get you far if it's followed by operational inadequacy. Think of it this way: Operational excellence is the foundation on which Strategic excellence is built.

The Capability Assessment Matrix

Consider the Capability Assessment Matrix of Figure 3, and "guesstimate" where you think your business currently sits.

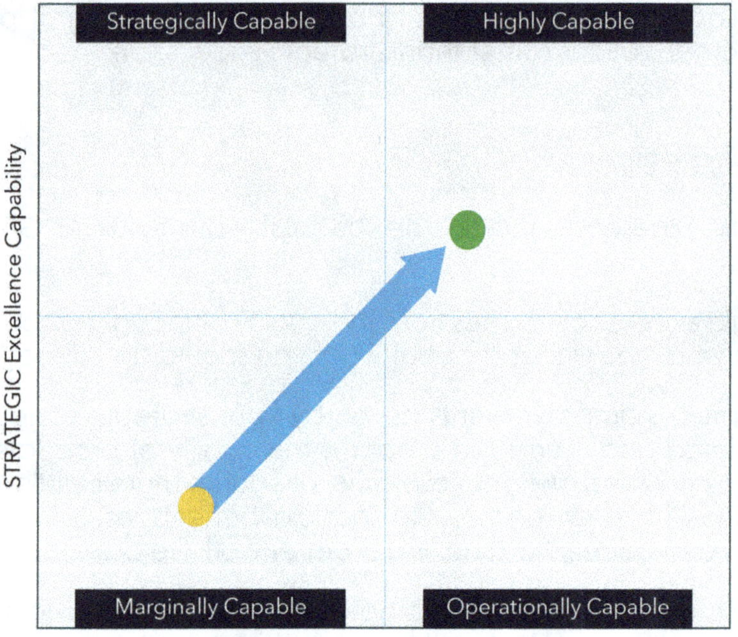

Figure 3: With the MBE approach, your transition to penetrate the Highly Capable quadrant will take about 2 years

Most SME business CEOs are only marginally capable of improving their business because they spend most of their time working IN the business rather than ON the business. When improvements are made, they tend to be reactive and ad hoc, without a structured implementation to ensure each improvement will last far beyond the current fire-fighting incident.

A strategically capable business is excellent at capitalizing on external opportunities to better position their business in the marketplace. This kind of business is usually led by a CEO or founder with a strong vision plus a growth orientation. However, practical execution of that vision via their strategic Objectives is often quite poor. That is because changing the business strategically usually requires simultaneous and significant changes to operations.

An operationally capable business is one that understands the importance of optimizing the delivery of their products or services through the organization's processes. However, these businesses often have tunnel vision. They are unable to adjust to outside opportunities and changes within their industry that may adversely impact their offerings or even their entire business model. These businesses may be successful one day and bankrupt the next, having been disrupted by an agile, fast moving competitor entering their industry.

No matter where your business currently sits on the 2 x 2 MBE Capability Assessment Matrix of Figure 3, moving into the Highly Capable quadrant will require a carefully considered, comprehensive and well-executed implementation.

A Capability Assessment Quiz is available on our website if you'd like to confirm where you sit. Check out Appendix A: Further Resources at the end of this book for details.

Four Common Reasons for Getting Started

For the past 30 years we have been presenting half-day public workshops for groups of CEOs, primarily sponsored by the international TEC (The Executive Connection) and Vistage networks and also sponsored by several Business Schools in Australia—particularly the Mt Eliza Centre for Executive Education (part of Melbourne University), Monash University in Melbourne, and the Macquarie Business School in Sydney. Through these high-profile education and awareness programs, the participating CEOs are exposed to a wide variety of business improvement techniques, not just ours. For decades, these workshop programs have been our main source of clients.

The CEO client feedback suggests four main reasons for engaging us to help them get started:

1. Their past attempts at implementing strategy have been poor. Day-to-day operational pressures prevented key people giving enough emphasis to executing the projects needed to deliver their Objectives in full.
2. They were unsure how to address disruptive technology challenges, particularly those involving new IT systems.
3. They liked the simple, holistic nature of our approach in addressing both strategic and operational aspects of their business simultaneously. They were unaware of any other approach that addressed all the critical issues as an integrated whole and in the right order.
4. They liked the idea that the approach didn't require copious and expensive amounts of external consulting input.

Do any of these catalysts for change apply to you?

The Business Excellence Comparison Matrix

If you're interested in business excellence, there is no shortage of options available to you. From the proven international frameworks for excellence to online influencers touting untested or unproven theories, there will always be more people offering you advice than you have time to implement, or even evaluate. As with almost everything in modern life, you're faced with a bewildering array of choices, an almost infinite menu of possibilities, and much of it of questionable quality.

The trick isn't in sourcing information on the topic of excellence. The challenge is to weed out the irrelevant, inaccurate, incomplete, misguided or simply unsuitable.

Let's compare the MBE approach to some other well-known business improvement approaches used by SMEs.

Table 1: A comparison of the MBE approach relative to other popular business improvement approaches

Approach	TQM with ISO 9000	Six Sigma	Lean	Agile & OKRs	Operational Excellence	MBE
Leadership and management of change built in at all levels from the outset	*	*	*	*	*	*
Customer-focused process modelling and process improvement techniques	*	*	*	*	*	*
Progressive engagement of all employees	*	*	*	*	*	*
Alignment of strategy, Objectives, and key performance indicators	*					*
Accountable, cross-functional Process Managers for all Key Processes	*		*		*	*
Iterative and incremental implementations of strategy via small, autonomous, cross-functional teams				*		*
Performance reporting framework for operations and strategy deployment	*		*	*		*
Cumulative tracking of net financial benefits of process improvement projects		*				*
Quality Management System (QMS) framework with knowledge flows linked to process flows	*	*	*		*	*
Step-by-step implementation guidelines for full business excellence						*

With reference to Table 1, here are some candid comments on the other competitive offerings relative to the MBE approach...

TQM with ISO 9000

This comes closest to the MBE approach for full business excellence. It has been around for at least 40 years. TQM is almost out of date in terms of contemporary business language, but the approach remains solid. Dr Rehn's involvement with TQM training in the 1980s played a big part in his formulation of the then embryonic MBE approach.

In TQM, deep attention is paid to the need for customer focus in business processes and the need to minimize process variation. It also is directly applicable to the deployment of business strategy down and across a business, but not to the formulation of that strategy.

TQM encompasses the achievement of ISO 9000 certification[6] for businesses that need it.

Dr. Rehn has been involved in translating the Japanese version of TQM into the Australian idiom to make TQM easier to implement in this country, Honda Australia being a case in point.

Six Sigma

Six Sigma[7] is a specialist methodology effecting process improvement by minimizing process variation using statistical process control. Internal or external people are trained to become qualified as expert practitioners ("Black Belt" and "Master Black Belt") or less expert practitioners ("Green Belt").

Six Sigma is often applied in manufacturing businesses producing volume product.

It is rarely used by service businesses due to its statistical complexity, the high overhead costs of training, plus the fact that service businesses are rarely involved in providing high volume repeatable offerings.

The Six Sigma methodology does nothing for strategy alignment and short-cycle, iterative implementation, or other aspects of the Agile approach for strategy deployment.

The good news is that many documented case studies done on Six Sigma around the world provide compelling evidence for the net financial benefits of process improvement. We have leveraged these proven results for process improvement in preparing the SME business case[11] for the much more comprehensive MBE approach to business excellence.

Lean

The Lean approach[8] is concerned with optimizing added value for customers by removing waste (i.e., non value-adding activities) from business processes through continuous improvement efforts. Lean has been particularly popular with manufacturing businesses as epitomized by Toyota over many decades. For maximum benefit, collaboration with other businesses involved in the target manufacturer's supply chain is required.

However, the Lean concept is relatively new to the service sector. Its introduction to service businesses started at the turn of this century.

There are two main aspects of Lean for a service business:

1. At a strategic level, Lean improves business performance by targeting and eliminating activities that that do not add value to the services on offer. However, Lean does not focus on strategy formulation or strategy execution.

2. At a more tactical level, Lean is a process optimization methodology aimed at reducing the cycle times required to execute repetitive processes.

As indicated in Table 1, the MBE approach does this and more, resulting in an integrated, holistic optimization for the entire business system. With the MBE approach, special emphasis is placed on tracking the cumulative net benefits of all process improvement projects.

Agile and OKRs

At the moment there is quite a buzz in the marketplace about Objective Key Results (OKRs) as the pathway for an organization to become Agile[9]. OKRs are essentially a strategic plan deployment mechanism that emerged from Silicon Valley. They were first used at Intel, but Google made them famous. A lot of leaner, fast-moving companies are now focused on using OKRs.

The problem is that they are often implemented poorly because the guidelines for how to set them up are quite vague. Nonetheless, a lot of people relate to them. Put simply, you start with a business Objective and then the key result is a type of measure that relates to that, much like a key performance indicator. An OKR is for a finite period such as a quarter, although the period may be extended if the Objective has not been achieved by the end of the quarter. OKRs can be applied to businesses, things, or departments. The ultimate aim is to cascade the strategic Objectives down and across the business to become responsibilities for local teams and individual employees in implementing those Objectives in a bottom up manner.

We strongly support the overall intent of OKRs which is to create and maintain an agile, fast-moving, top-to-bottom strategic alignment of a business. However, where the OKR approach is deficient is in providing guidance on how to *formulate* the long-term business strategy that yields those Objectives. In our conversations with CEOs who use OKRs extensively within their business, the number one complaint we hear is the difficulty of identifying and specifying which OKRs matter and how they align with business strategy.

Our approach to formulating a 1-page Strategic Plan with a maximum of seven Objectives is a very effective way of identifying what the top level OKRs should be. Using a simple selection technique, we then cascade these Objectives down into quarterly projects with specified deliverables for local autonomous teams.

There is also some confusion in the marketplace over whether Key Results (the KR of OKR) or KPIs (Key Performance Indicators) should be the prime metrics for strategy deployment via the quarterly projects. We avoid this confusion by using KPIs exclusively and by providing clear guidance for how and when they should be formulated throughout the business whenever business performance needs to be measured (i.e., not only for strategy deployment but also for operations).

For the above reasons, we do not refer to OKRs at all in the MBE approach.

Operational Excellence

As explained earlier in Part 1, Operational excellence is only half the game of full business excellence – the other half being Strategic excellence.

This is why the Operational Excellence column of Table 1 is only half full of included business excellence features.

Each row of the comparison matrix of Table 1 describes an essential feature of full business excellence. Let's briefly consider each feature in turn...

Leadership and Management of Change Built In at All Levels from the Outset

When implemented well, all six listed business improvement approaches have this essential feature.

Autocratic, top-down management systems which implement change from above without grass-roots support are doomed to fail. Similarly, change from the bottom up that fails to secure support at the highest levels within the company will likely flounder.

We were once engaged by the CEO of an Australian camping supplies company to facilitate their strategic plan as the precursor to full implementation of the MBE approach. A day or so before the scheduled Workshop, the CEO announced that he would be unable to attend the workshop because he had to attend a meeting in Singapore. He suggested that the workshop go ahead in his absence.

We held the 2-day workshop and the 15 participants were excited about the agreed direction for the business and were looking forward to execution of the strategy.

A few days later, the CEO returned, reviewed the plan and bluntly stated that he had no intention of following that route. He immediately cancelled the plan and its execution. The workshop participants had been empowered to develop the strategy, but enthusiasm for their planned future was dashed instantly. Their faith in the concept of an empowered workforce took a severe beating that day.

Business strategy should never be developed in the absence of leadership and direct input from the CEO. Nor should it be decided at the highest levels and then not shared with the rest of the workforce. Neither is a route to business excellence.

Customer-Focused Process Modelling and Process Improvement Techniques

In the past, a company's product had to be better than the competition's product. Today however, your customer's experience must be better than the customer experience offered by the competition. And the way to improve the customer experience is to improve the processes that contribute to that customer experience. Not surprisingly, all six listed approaches for business improvement address the importance of this essential feature.

Amazon, IKEA and Apple exemplify how to deliver products fast and with seamless service. SMEs need to do likewise. Customer delight fuels word of mouth referrals, and when amplified by clever use of social media it can generate outstanding returns.

Being small is no excuse for providing poor customer service. SMEs need to ensure that all their policies and procedures target and secure a seamless customer experience that is positive and repeatable.

Progressive Engagement of All Employees

This is the third and last feature that is common to all six listed business improvement approaches.

We once were engaged by a CEO who inherited a large business. Sadly, he had a personal leadership style that was extremely toxic. He micro-managed everything. While he understood the business financials to the nth degree, his inter-personal skills left much to be desired and so several senior staff members had become disempowered.

We terminated our involvement with the company following facilitation of its business strategy. It was clear that full implementation of the plan would at best be slow and at worst impossible due to the adverse impact the CEO was having on his peoples' willingness to participate. A few key employees subsequently left for greener pastures elsewhere.

Business excellence requires positive buy-in and participation by all employees.

Alignment of Strategy, Objectives, and Key Performance Indicators

Three of the six approaches fail to feature this aspect of business excellence.

A sound strategy creates top-down alignment that cascades to every level of a business. It enables top-down initiatives while also triggering bottom-up process improvements initiated by employees at the coalface of your business.

Your Objectives describe what your business seeks to deliver over the planning period. The targets you set for the associated KPIs let you know if you're on track for their delivery in full.

The aim here is to align your Objectives with your long-term vision for the business and eliminate anything that is counterproductive. The strategy should be widely shared down and across your organization and must be easy to keep up to date.

Accountable, Cross-Functional Process Managers for All Key Processes

Two of the six approaches fail to include this crucial aspect of business excellence.

Part-time Process Managers have cross-functional responsibilities. They take ownership of a key process from end to end, even if parts of the process are operationally handled by other organizational units. Much like a Health and Safety Officer, or a First Aider, they take on full accountability for improvement in one major component of the business. It is vital that they take their part-time role seriously and that their role is clearly understood and appreciated by the entire organization.

Often, we come across managers who put their day-to-day operational responsibilities first and consider their process management role as an optional extra. From the outset, their Process Manager role needs to become part of the working culture. Working ON the business through their assigned key process(es) is just as important as working normally IN the business as the line manager of their own organizational unit.

Process Managers help you avoid getting yourself caught up in the classic "Who's job is it?" dilemma, embodied by the joke:

> *"This is a story about four people named Everybody, Somebody, Anybody, and Nobody. There was an important job to be done and Everybody was sure that Somebody would do it. Anybody could have done it, but Nobody did it. Somebody got angry about that because it was Everybody's job. Everybody thought that Anybody could do it, but Nobody realized that Everybody wouldn't do it. In the end, Everybody blamed Somebody when Nobody did what Anybody could have done."*

Iterative and Incremental Implementations of Strategy by Small, Autonomous, Cross-Functional Teams

Four of the six approaches fail to feature this component of business excellence.

From Agile, we take the importance of iterative and incremental execution of strategy via quarterly projects done by small autonomous teams of willing part-time participants. The MBE approach places heavy emphasis on the power and use of such teams and projects triggered by the need to progress a strategic Objective or to overcome an operational weakness.

Why small teams? Because too many cooks spoil the broth. Small teams encourage speed of execution, and there are less management overheads involved. You can't afford to involve everyone in every project, even if they all wanted to be.

Why autonomous teams? Here's an adage worth considering: "Tell someone what to do or how to do it, but not both." Tasks can be assigned, but accountability for their execution cannot be enforced. At the end of the day, accountability is an act of will. Autonomous teams encourage this positive behavior.

Lack of accountability can be a big obstacle for team effectiveness. Over the years we have witnessed many teams where the leader (i.e., the Project Manager) tries to hold their team members accountable. By contrast, in high performing teams, the team members hold *each other* accountable.

When a team focuses on achieving the result together, they are more likely to hold each other accountable. Well-coached sports teams epitomize this behavior. Every member of the team is working towards the same goal—to win the game. Individual recognition for performance is set aside for the benefit of the team.

During the 1990s, IBM reinforced the need for peer group accountability by listing the following requirement in its top six behavioral guidelines for employees: "We always keep the promises we make to each other." As a former employee of IBM Global Services for five years, Dr Rehn can attest to the positive impact of this behavior. For example, when requests for assistance were made from Australia to New York or Chicago, that assistance was always forthcoming—and quickly.

Similarly, members of local IBM teams in Australia were careful when making their promises because they knew that the other team members would hold them accountable.

When we worked with an offshoot of the global pharmaceutical company Eli Lilly and Co. in Australia, their behavioral mantra was: "Together and from each our best." This, too, overtly encouraged peer group accountability for the betterment of the organization.

Performance Reporting Framework for Operations and Strategy Deployment

Two of the six approaches fail to feature this aspect of business excellence.

It is highly desirable to have a performance reporting framework that encompasses the collection and reporting of the key operational and strategic metrics for a finite period, thereby ensuring that Process Managers and Project Managers remain fully accountable.

A huge range of software is available that offers reporting features for businesses. Some businesses will already have made a considerable investment in such software. It makes sense to leverage what you already have available, provided it meets the requirements of your chosen approach to business transformation.

Cumulative Tracking of Net Financial Benefits of Process Improvement Projects

Four of the six approaches fail to feature this aspect of business excellence.

Many CEOs and managers are skeptical about the value of process improvement techniques—until they quantify and track the cumulative net benefits of completed projects. This is why we make it easy to keep track and report progress of all projects via a quantified graphical summary of the results.

Quality Management System (QMS) Framework with Knowledge Flows Linked to Process Flows

It is imperative that the business keeps its entire process collection up to date every month. This is the collective responsibility of the Process Managers for all the Key Processes of the business.

The up-to-date process collection becomes the core of the organization's ever-improving QMS – i.e., the reference system for everyone within the business who needs to know how things should best be done for any key process or sub-process.

Five of the six business improvement approaches usually include a QMS that captures process flows well. (The only one that doesn't is Agile and OKRs). However, the idea of adding important knowledge flows to the documented process flows of a QMS is relatively new. These days, software is available that makes it easy to append any digital knowledge artefact (such as a spreadsheet or video) to any individual process step in a digital flowchart. We strongly encourage this technique.

Step-By-Step Implementation Guidelines for Full Business Excellence

Only the MBE approach features this aspect of business excellence. It is why we wrote this book. Because SMEs are less likely to have business excellence facilitation skills on staff, we offer detailed step-by-step implementation guidelines for full business excellence.

Over past decades, we have taken the best bits of the various improvement techniques designed for larger businesses, and simplified them to form an approach that's practical and logically prescriptive for any SME.

Problems with International Frameworks for Business Excellence

The MBE approach is holistic and focuses on doing things in the right order. The 80 or so current international frameworks[10] are also holistic, each with 7-9 common criteria that we agree with. However, we simplify and integrate these 7-9 criteria to form just five all-encompassing Prerequisites for full business excellence. This makes the criteria more accessible and memorable for SMEs. In a comprehensive employee survey during the late 1990s, IBM found that most of their people had difficulty remembering 7 or more things in any important list. The five Prerequisites are:

- Process Design & Improvement
- Shared Strategic Direction
- Performance Measurement & Feedback
- Knowledge Capture & Leverage
- Leadership & Management of Change

All the current international frameworks are designed to help businesses *measure* how well they are performing against their 7-9 criteria for excellence. Unfortunately, they are devoid of guidelines on how best to *implement* their stated criteria. Instead, each participating business is simply encouraged to undertake an up-front assessment of current performance against each of the criteria and is then left to conceive and implement a project to ameliorate the exposed biggest area of weakness.

Then it's "rinse and repeat", choosing and implementing the next priority project with constant reference back to the full assessment results. The assessment may be repeated every year or so to check on progress.

It's an approach that slowly builds capability across all the criteria. There are two fundamental problems with this:

1. It focuses attention on your business weaknesses, which can be demoralizing, especially when the reward for improvement is to switch focus to the next-weakest link.
2. It takes 4-5 years to make substantial improvement against all the criteria.

In stark contrast, the MBE approach gives you a fast start with early gains. Critical mass is progressively reached across all five Prerequisites within just two years. From then on, you simply consolidate what you have learned and reap the rapidly compounding net benefits.

Our initial implementation phase configures every Prerequisite within the first 12 weeks, and then we put the structure in place to start making progress on all fronts. The key to maximizing the positive impact is to do the right things in the right order, making sure that there are no unintended consequences.

This approach generates a comparatively fast return on investment in terms of both time and money.

If you have a particularly small business (e.g., with only 10 or so full-time employees), you may need to modify the implementation to take a little longer than 2 years due to the scarcity of available people resources in the early stages.

Our research into the take-up rate of the international frameworks suggests that the effective market penetration of business excellence in SMEs globally is only about 1-2%. We believe the main reasons why the international reference frameworks are not popular among SMEs today may be summarized as follows:

1. The 7-9 criteria are difficult to remember and so are not fixed in the minds of managers or employees when making day-to-day decisions.

2. A comprehensive self-assessment against the criteria and the many listed requirements for each is required up front before beginning practical implementation. This takes too much time and effort for no immediate return.

3. Based on the initial self-assessment, project-by-project implementations are implicitly recommended, and this means 4-5 years are needed to make substantial impact on all the criteria.

4. All the frameworks advocate integration, but there are no instructions for how to link the criteria and the requirements for each to form an integrated whole. Furthermore, there are no instructions for ensuring that the series of completed projects result in seamless processes across the business.

5. Registering and seeking a formal national award for outstanding performance against the criteria can be a distraction from the main goal of building excellence capability.

SMEs are different

SMEs cannot simply be treated as small versions of large businesses because they have unique characteristics. Here are some of them:

1. They often have limited financial resources to invest in new ways of doing things.

2. Most employee training is unstructured, ad-hoc, and in-house, delivered with little or no professional support staff.

3. Owners / CEOs / Managers often spend most of their time working IN the business, with little time to work ON the business.

4. Owners / CEOs / Managers often try to control every aspect of the business and fail to delegate enough.

5. Immature or irrelevant processes and ineffective IT support systems often result in reactive firefighting when things go wrong.

6. A top-down, hierarchical approach to strategy deployment is often aggravated by the inability to allocate resources flexibly and swiftly across organizational unit boundaries to where they are needed most.

The international frameworks ought to be amended and adapted to serve the true needs and circumstances of SMEs, but so far this is not happening to an extent sufficient to make them truly useful. The main concession for SMEs to date is that the initial assessment has been simplified and can be done by the business itself rather than by hired specialists.

This is why we have developed our own MBE Reference Framework and MBE approach for pragmatic implementation in SMEs.

Cost of Inaction

One Australian construction company we worked with faced going out of business unless things were turned around quickly. At the time, a large proportion of their steel fabrication workforce was idle because insufficient work had been won due to a string of lost tenders. Worse, their sales pipeline going forward was far too small to sustain the business for much longer.

The trigger for them adopting the MBE approach was the need to urgently reengineer their sales process. Once that was done and the level of sold work began to increase markedly, they moved to adopt the rest of the approach.

While this is an example of a company in desperate need of process improvements just to stay afloat, even for businesses which on the surface are doing well there's a hidden cost of lost opportunity through inaction to improve things. If you're doing well now with ad hoc and informal processes, just imagine how much better you might become if you had everything organized and documented as a result of systematic process improvement.

Hundreds of documented case studies from around the world confirm that over a 5-year period, those companies that engage in a comprehensive process improvement program realize *cumulative* financial *net* savings of about +22.5% of their annual Sales Revenue measured at the *beginning* of the 5-year period[11].

How would you like to realize a +22.5% increase in your company's financial performance? What would that mean for the company's bank balance? Consider how your decision to target inefficiencies, remedy them, and hence improve the company's financial performance by +22.5% would be celebrated by your shareholders and potentially result in increased salaries and bonuses for you and your colleagues.

Do take a moment to do the calculation for your business: **Cumulative Net Savings over the next 5 years = at least 22.5% x your *Current* annual Sales Revenue.**

This is also the cost of inaction if you decide to do nothing. How would your shareholders feel if they became aware of the company's inefficiencies limiting their return on investment? How would it look if they also discovered that their Management Team had consciously decided NOT to embrace this outstanding opportunity to improve the company's processes and its bottom line?

Of course, inaction is always an option, but clearly a very expensive one. After all, excellence is not compulsory, and success is not mandatory. An ongoing opportunity cost of this magnitude is not sustainable in today's highly competitive marketplace.

But wait, there's more! While Operational excellence alone can generate these outstanding net savings, Strategic excellence can increase your company's net benefits even more. It will unleash your company's full potential and increase your company's resilience in a rapidly changing marketplace.

Inefficiency is a thief of your company's true potential, of your employees' healthy work-life balance, of your shareholders' returns, and of your own success as an industry leader.

Without a coherent strategy, your business will not have a set of challenging but achievable Objectives. The focus needed to deliver on those Objectives via proactive action will therefore be absent. Without sound planning, it's difficult to budget for the personnel and funding resources necessary to develop and launch new products or services and grow the business. The adage: "Failing to plan is planning to fail," often attributed to Ben Franklin, applies.

For example, Kodak's story of failing[12] has its roots in its success, which made it resistant to change. They believed their strength lay in their brand and marketing. Even though they were one of the first companies to develop a digital camera, they underestimated the threat of digital technology and the changing focus of consumer needs to their existing business. At its peak, Kodak held about 90% of the US film market and was one of the world's most recognizable and valuable brands. It failed to plan for the transition and paid the ultimate price in 2012 when it went out of business.

What is the lesson for SMEs from the Kodak experience? Just this: Every business needs to adjust to the emerging requirements of its customers—and this requires the strategic plan to keep the business relevant, even if it means competing against its own past strengths. Disrupt yourself before someone else does it for you!

One of our clients is a manufacturing and distribution company in Melbourne Australia. They make rubber and plastic components for vibration control and engine suspensions in automotive manufacturing. However, when General Motors-Holden, Toyota, and Mitsubishi all ceased manufacturing vehicles in Australia a few years ago, this local manufacturer faced a bleak future for providing each of them with specialist parts.

Had they done nothing about strategic planning in the face of dramatically falling revenue, they would have run the risk of going out of business. Through aggressive strategic planning and execution, they have become successful in morphing their business towards the design and manufacture of products for the automotive *aftermarket*, plus a new suite of products for apparel trimmings.

They are now regarded as an innovation leader in light-weight materials technology for the automotive sector. This success would not have happened had they decided to do nothing in the face of changed circumstances.

Cost of Poor Quality (COPQ)

The Cost of Poor Quality (COPQ)[13] is a revealing metric for overall business performance. There is a direct and inverse correlation between the size of COPQ and financial performance.

COPQ is the price your business pays when a service or product is not perfect. It is an outcome of all the processes covering the creation and distribution of said product or service. COPQ includes all the visible plus hidden costs that would disappear if your systems, processes, products, and services were perfect.

For over half a century, many businesses around the world have used various and overlapping transformational techniques (including TQM, Lean Thinking, Six Sigma, and other process improvement techniques) to reduce their total COPQ.

As shown in Figure 4, the idea is to invest time and effort in *prevention* of process problems in order save a much bigger amount of money dealing with internal and external process failures.

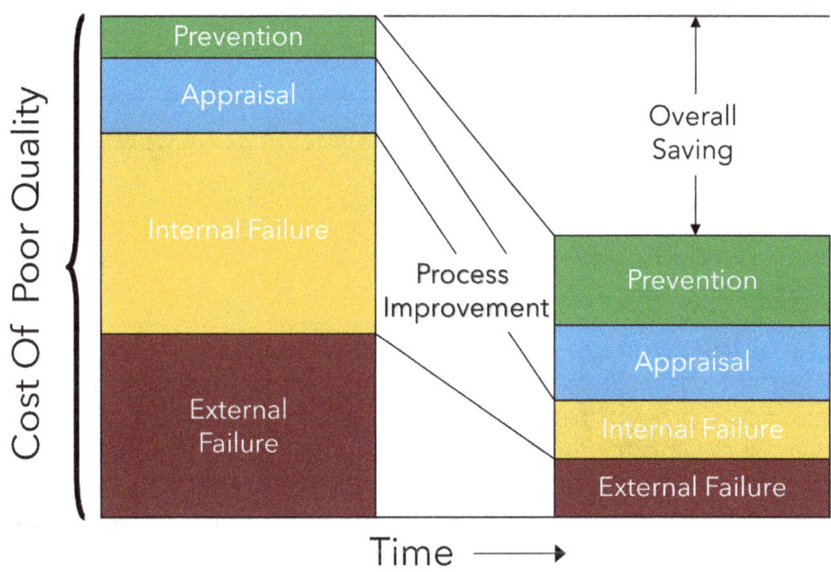

Figure 4: Reducing the total Cost of Poor Quality through process improvement

Our experience and that of others has resulted in three realizations:

1. COPQ is always much larger than the visible costs shown in the accounts.
2. COPQ is larger for complex businesses such as manufacturing where there are many value-adding steps and dependencies on other businesses in the supply chain.
3. Although much (but not all) of COPQ is avoidable, few businesses have clear responsibilities for action to reduce it dramatically with a structured approach for doing so.

As a result of 30 years of implementation around the globe, Six Sigma practitioners have reached a consensus on the size of COPQ relative to sales for low, average and high performing businesses[11]:

Table 2: Average COPQ as a percentage of Sales

Sigma Level	Defects Per Million Opportunities (DPMO)	Yield	COPQ as % Sales
6	3.4	99.9997%	<10%
5	233	99.976%	10-15%
4	**6,210**	**99.4%**	**15-20%**
3	**66,807**	**93%**	**20-30%**
2	308,537	69%	30-40%
1	691,000	31%	>40%

Based on the "guesstimated" yield of your organization's current delivery system (column 3), you can now quantify the approximate size of your COPQ as % Sales (column 4). Average businesses are at Sigma Level 3.

The size of the average organization's COPQ, which includes the invisible costs as well as the visible costs, is clearly enormous. The invisible costs are not represented in your financial accounts, but you are still paying for them. Examples of invisible costs include loss of a customer, poor staff utilization, poor staff morale, unempowered employees, rework, and excessive hand-offs between process steps.

Examples of visible costs (i.e., in your accounts) include such things as: excessive inventory, scrapped materials, servicing of complaints, fixing warranty claims, and addressing legal challenges.

Realizing the total Cost of Poor Quality in a business can be quite a shock for its managers.

Case Study for Cost of Poor Quality: Philmac

Philmac develops, manufactures, and markets fluid transfer solutions for Australia and targeted export markets.

The company is a world leader in the design, manufacture, marketing and distribution of innovative, high-quality valves and fittings for pipeline systems and irrigation products. It has an unrelenting commitment to continuous improvement in a work environment which encourages people to develop their creativity, initiative, and confidence.

In August 2006, the company engaged the Henly Management Group to undertake a comprehensive Cost of Poor Quality (COPQ) Review based on the annualized year-to-date costs as at the end of June 2006. The scope of the review covered the following functional business units:

- Administration and Finance
- Human Resources
- Regional Sales
- Australian Sales & Distribution/National Sales
- Marketing
- Customer Service
- Export (Excluding the UK)
- Product Development
- Quality
- Supply
- Production
- Distribution

The review found that the overall COPQ was $11.8M and this represented 25% of the overall cost structure.

The Costs of Prevention were $4.7M (40% of COPQ) and the Costs of Failure (internal + external) were $5.1M (43% of COPQ).

These values were considered to be disproportionately high. A major conclusion was that the high cost Prevention activities were not particularly effective at reducing the costs of failure.

The results of the COPQ review and supporting interview process suggested that the improvement opportunity available to Philmac in the short-to-medium term (12-18 months) was to reduce the overall COPQ down to $9.7M against the base line of $11.8M.

In the medium-to-longer term (18 months - 3 years,) the aim was to further reduce the overall COPQ to $6.8M against the base line of $11.8M, and then to continue to improve even further on this as part of an ongoing process improvement culture that should be established by then.

The three recommended mechanisms for achieving this were:

1. Implementation of statistical based approaches to quality control (increasing appraisal costs, but reducing failure) including acceptance sampling and statistical process control

2. Introduction of a formal and structured approach to continuous improvement through team-based problem solving and embedding it into the culture

3. Implementing improved coordination mechanisms between organizational "silos" to decrease "bullwhip effects" in the supply chain

The basic thrust of improvement activities pursued by improvement teams would be the elimination of external failure and reduction of internal failure through improvements in appraisal and more effective prevention, plus the elimination of ineffective prevention.

Shortly thereafter in 2007, the then Managing Director (from 2003-2012), Chris Stathy decided to introduce the MBE approach to aid the company in implementing these recommendations.

> *"We engaged with Mark Rehn (My Business Excellence) in 2007 to guide us through what was to become a significant transformation of our approach to quality improvement at Philmac.*
>
> *Even though Philmac was a well-established, high performance manufacturer, the Henly review revealed significant opportunities that if addressed would ensure Philmac's competitiveness and sustainability well into the future.*
>
> *By applying the MBE approach with Mark's guidance, our leadership team was able to fully appreciate the value and importance of adopting the COPQ principles. Embracing this resulted in an entire culture shift throughout the business.*
>
> *This was an exciting time at Philmac with specific COPQ projects being undertaken across our supply chain and customer service activities. These projects resulted in real value to the bottom line both in terms of cost and quality performance*

improvements. I am sure the MBE approach remains entrenched in the Philmac DNA to this day."

Chris Stathy OAM, Director, Hazelwood Industry Solutions

If you would like to determine the actual Cost of Poor Quality for your business, the procedure for doing so is set out in the Australian Standard AS 2561:2010.[14]

Qualitative Benefits of Action

Throughout 2011 and 2012, The Mt Eliza Centre for Executive Education (part of Melbourne University's Business School) conducted a professional development program. It was designed specifically for the CEOs/Owners/Managers of SMEs in Victoria and New South Wales who were members of Enterprise Connect, an Australian Government initiative backed by industry. It offers comprehensive advice and support to eligible Australian businesses to help them transform and reach their full potential.

During those two years, the program titled "Leadership 21" was run seven times, with a different cohort of 20+ participants each time. A total of 168 SMEs undertook the program which also connected participants with the network of other participating owner managers.

As a precursor to the program design, the Mt Eliza team and Enterprise Connect wanted to ensure it had a deep and thorough understanding of the needs and priorities of the target audience. This involved several research and consultation activities. Included was extensive research into similar programs offered in other countries, namely: Lancaster University's LEAD Program in the UK and ICEHOUSE'S ICEBRIDGE Owner Manager Program in New Zealand.

Also included was a review of research and documentation on Australian SMEs plus a review of lessons learned from Mt Eliza's own Owner Manager Program which was run several years earlier.

The findings led to identification of four development priorities for the target participant group:

- Strategic planning and implementation
- Leading business change and growth
- Managing and engaging the workforce
- Resilience and flexibility

It was recognized that sound planning and implementation of strategy would naturally need to address the other three priorities.

With the need for integration in mind, Mt Eliza chose the MBE approach for practical implementation of business excellence to form a key thread throughout each of the seven iterations of the Leadership 21 Program.

Over the 4 residential Workshops (total 10 days) conducted over 9 consecutive months, with critical prework in between, participants reported significant changes to their businesses and leadership performance, with the skills they learned being transferred instantly to their businesses. They finished the program feeling more confident and better equipped to grow and develop their businesses further.

Figure 5 shows the journey undertaken during and between these workshops.

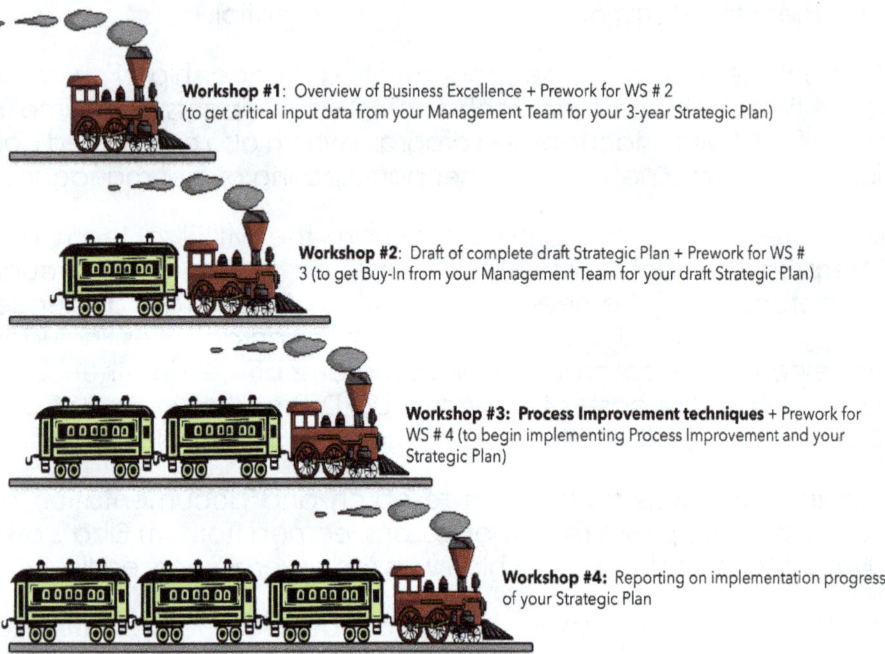

Workshop #1: Overview of Business Excellence + Prework for WS # 2
(to get critical input data from your Management Team for your 3-year Strategic Plan)
Workshop #2: Draft of complete draft Strategic Plan + Prework for WS # 3 (to get Buy-In from your Management Team for your draft Strategic Plan)
Workshop #3: Process Improvement techniques + Prework for WS # 4 (to begin implementing Process Improvement and your Strategic Plan)
Workshop #4: Reporting on implementation progress of your Strategic Plan

Figure 5: The Business Excellence journey built momentum over 9 months

According to Mt Eliza:

> *"Past participants reported business growth, higher revenue, increased profitability and improved work-life balance, among other positive outcomes."*

The Mt Eliza Leadership 21 Program was run again in 2015-2016 with increased government funding and was open to SMEs based anywhere in Australia.

The Mt Eliza program typifies the qualitative benefits of implementing business excellence. Time after time, CEOs, managers, and even employees who have taken part in the MBE approach tell us they feel empowered. They feel they can implement change within the business and make a difference. Rather than saying: "It's broken!" they feel they can action real change to improve their business. They report a better work-life balance. Instead of being tense at work and worrying about what's not working or being criticized, they can now make their processes work smoothly, and still go home at five o'clock and see their family.

Another qualitative benefit is alignment and visibility. Often, we meet SME managers, CEOs or owners who hold on too tightly to decision-making and don't delegate well. There's a consequential lack of visibility as to what they are trying to do with respect to company direction. This leaves employees feeling alienated and confused.

Once we show them how to get things working by implementing the MBE approach, the lines of communication are opened. There's visibility of what they are trying to achieve. They have alignment throughout the business. Everyone understands not just what they are doing but why, and they are all pulling in the same direction.

It all comes back to the ability to make a difference. Employees have a purpose beyond simply "doing their job".

Quantitative Benefits of Action—The Financial Net Benefits

We have already talked about the financial benefits in relation to the Cost of Inaction. The flip side of that is obviously the gains that can be realized by taking action. You will recall that the net financial benefits of implementing Operational excellence well over the next five years amount to at least +22.5% of *this* year's annual Sales[11].

It is important to realize that the net benefits of implementing Strategic excellence are *in addition* to those generated by Operational excellence. Although the financial net benefits of Strategic excellence are usually substantial, they are notoriously difficult to forecast. Strategic excellence is influenced by a host of variables. Every business responds differently according to its own unique set of top-down and bottom-up strategic initiatives and the way in which it executes them.

While the benefits of strategic excellence are impossible to predict due to the uniqueness of each company's approach, well-implemented strategic initiatives usually yield substantial top line (revenue) increases as well as bottom line (profit) increases. Certainly, the net benefits are well worth the effort.

As is the case for Operational excellence, the costs of doing nothing for Strategic excellence, though difficult to forecast, are substantial.

Now that you understand why you need the MBE approach to help you transform your business performance, let's consider your readiness for getting started.

Are You Ready?

One of the biggest issues in change management and business improvement, particularly for SMEs, is the danger of losing momentum.

A company CEO once engaged us to run a strategy workshop. He attended the workshop and appeared to be involved. Initially, there were no obvious issues. We progressed through the first four weeks of setting the foundation for full business excellence. Then, at the first monthly review meeting, as we were about to review their KPIs and plan their subsequent actions, the CEO stood up, said: "I'm not convinced by any of this," and walked out.

While this is an extreme example of losing momentum early on and throwing in the towel due to unfulfilled expectations for whatever reason, it's far from a unique story. We regularly hear about the inability of businesses to make improvements that stick.

Almost all businesses know they need to improve, but one of three things happen:

1. They have a strategy, but it hasn't been executed successfully.
2. They start an initiative to improve some aspect of their business but don't finish, and so never realize the net benefits.
3. They complete some process improvement projects and see the benefits in the short term, but the people involved later regress in part or whole to the old way of doing things.

As a result, there's a lingering sense of frustration at not being able to get the business to where they want it to be. The people in charge know a lot of the things that need to happen, but they just don't know where to start and how to progress efficiently.

Much of this is because they are too busy working IN the business instead of ON the business. They are often working flat out with no spare capacity. Faced with constant crises and demands, they're on that cliff edge, with the fire at their backs, and no parachute or hang glider to save them.

CEO Commitment

A strong commitment by the CEO is necessary for successful business transformation.

There's no getting away from it. No matter how much your business needs to change, and no matter how much you could benefit from the MBE approach, there's work involved for the CEO. There's the combined financial, time, and energy cost involved in following through. Never mind that the cost of NOT following through would be much higher.

The number one reason why most businesses don't transform themselves for the better is a lack of commitment and confidence in creating a climate of change at the very top of the tree[15]. The attitude of the CEO towards the growth of the business is paramount. If you're not in it with both feet, how can you expect your people to be?

Many years ago, when we were first thinking about having a website for MBE, we were asked to define our ideal type of potential client—our "avatar". Who are we trying to reach? Our response was, and still is, that the website user, and reader of this book, needs to be ambitious, growth-oriented and serious about building the best possible business. In short, they are going all in, while doing everything possible to ensure their people are also going all in.

We are definitely not interested in working with the many contented CEOs and Management Teams who argue: "We're doing okay. We made a profit last year. Why should we bother?"

It's a process of self-selection and self-identification. If you recognize yourself in the first description above, we're here to help you.

But if, in your heart, you resonate more with the second description, that's okay, too. You may have some work to do on yourself before you try to lead your business to become excellent at what it does. Alternatively, the MBE approach may just not be for you.

Collective Leadership Style of the Management Team

The second requirement for successful transformation is the collective leadership style of your Management Team.

As indicated in Figure 6, since you want employee behaviors aligned to the steady improvement of the business, you need to ensure that the primary orientation of the collective leadership style is more towards humble Coaches and Enablers rather than egocentric Directors and Heroes.

Leadership Style

Director	Hero	Coach	Enabler
Does *TO* others Master	Does *FOR* others All knowing provider	Does *WITH* others Expert and teacher	Does *THROUGH* others Facilitator and mentor
Unquestioning followers Follow the rules	Passive recipients Step aside	**Learning participants** **Apply the learning**	**Self learners; Self starters** **Find new ways**

Induced Behaviour

Myron Tribus

Figure 6: Leadership styles have enormous impact on employee behavior

In his seminal study of "Good to Great" companies in the United States, Professor Jim Collins[16] also confirmed that a humble leadership style is needed at the very top (CEO) of the organization—while paradoxically combined with an iron-hard will to get the right things done "no matter what".

He also found that each of the "Great" companies had a CEO leader who first got the right people on the bus before deciding where the bus needed to go via their Shared Strategic Direction. Of course, this is not always a possibility for an existing business.

Therefore, it may be prudent for you and other members of your Management Team to assess where each currently sits on the above spectrum of leadership styles, and then support each other to make conscious efforts to shift the collective leadership style to the right.

If you're like the CEO we mentioned earlier who insisted on micro-managing everything, you need to consider giving up an element of control if you wish to empower your workforce to make decisions, be keen to learn and be keen to improve processes within their own sphere of influence.

Case Study: Intrepid Travel and the Intrepid Group

Throughout this book, we will be using Intrepid Travel and the Intrepid Group as a case study to illustrate the effectiveness of the overall MBE implementation process. Fortunately, the chairman of the Intrepid Group, Darrell Wade, has long been ambitious both in terms of growth for the business and in terms of making a difference to the world. He also has a strong leadership style that is the opposite of autocratic—more a Coaching and Enabling leadership style. The leadership style of Intrepid's other co-founder, Jeff Manchester, is similar. Together, they own the business.

Over the years, they have deliberately recruited and developed a Management Team that reflects their own leadership styles and values.

Reflecting their desire to make a difference in the world, the company has been carbon-neutral since 2010. They also have a charity foundation which to 2019 has accrued $6M by the company matching all donations made by travelers and staff.

Intrepid's employees are empowered by the collective leadership style of the company. It's not surprising that Intrepid has become highly successful in applying the MBE approach over many years. More on the Intrepid story later.

Link between Trust and Empowerment

So, you won't get process management, accountability, and execution of fast process improvements with autonomous cross-functional teams if you can't support and trust your own people. You can coach and guide, but your business is not going to be as successful, agile, or able to scale if every decision has to be run up the flagpole for approval and intervention by management.

Trust also Needed at Lower Levels of Management—especially Supervisors

Going back some fifteen years, we had a client who was about to sack one of their supervisors. The client was a large paper manufacturing company. The person in the firing line was an autocratic supervisor of a local production team. Whenever anyone suggested improving the area under his control, he did everything possible to shut down the idea. His attitude was:

> *"How dare you challenge my role? I've been doing this for 32 years. I know what I'm doing. I'm going to retire within a few years and I'm going to keep doing things my way."*

We decided to give him one last chance; to be on a team to improve a small part of "his" process. After much grumbling and complaint, we finally convinced him to give it a go and to act simply as the "Subject Matter Expert" and member of the small team.

To our surprise, that person quickly became the lead facilitator in that company for change and process improvement until he retired three years later. Sometimes, all it takes is to experience one simple process improvement project to see and feel how powerful and empowering it can be for all concerned.

A Common Misconception

The biggest misconception we face with some CEOs considering embarking on the MBE approach is that this is all going to be easy.

It isn't. If it was easy, everyone would be doing it.

We do everything we can to make the process as painless as possible for everyone. We can simplify the system, spell out the techniques and processes to use, and can even support you through coaching if you so wish. But at the end of the day, you and your entire team have to be prepared to work ON your business as seriously as you work IN it for an extended period, ideally forever. Kaizen, remember, is the process of continuous and never-ending improvement towards perfection. It's not a weekend retreat to put out the fire, and then get back to business as usual.

So, there is a considerable amount of work your business must do to be the best it can possibly be. To think otherwise would be naive.

We are pragmatic when we talk about the workloads involved. Every employee should spend 5% of their time, on average, working on process improvement within their local area. For Process Managers and Project Managers, that rises to about 10% or a half-day per week. In the early stages, devoting slightly more time to kick-start the implementation is desirable.

As for the CEO, in the early days you may need to focus on the implementation for a full day per week. Over time, that reduces to about 6 hours per week. The promotion of business excellence and process improvement is your job first and foremost. If you don't give it that level of priority, no one else will take it seriously.

If the prospect of having your key employees devote half a day every week to process improvement fills you with fear that the "real" work won't get done, then you need MBE more than most. If everyone in your company is working flat out just to keep up, that's not a badge of honor, or something to be proud of. It's a clear sign that you may be one crisis away from closure and that you need to fix both your priorities and your processes.

Fortunately, we don't just *tell* you that your key people need to work ON your business for half a day per week. We also give you and them a clear pathway for getting to where that's possible. We help you put the structure in place at the beginning for fast process improvements aimed at simultaneously reducing their wasted time and raising their efficiency.

Making the right choices for Process Managers and identifying the right Operational and Strategic KPIs within the first few weeks dramatically increase the likelihood of successful continuation. These critical ingredients are easy to get wrong at the first attempt. We therefore recommend reviewing and finalizing those choices during the first three months. During that time, all the Process Managers are trained in their new part-time role, including how to choose and sponsor quarterly Projects. All members of the Management Team are trained in the simple techniques for Fast Process Improvement (FPI) and then participate in completing one FPI Project over the standard 8-week implementation period—so that later they can lead by example having personally experienced the FPI techniques in action.

By doing all the above during the first three months, you create forward momentum.

Change is hard. There will be times when it hurts. When you're super busy, it's easy to stop doing something important to address something urgent. To stop focusing on something that has long-term benefits, and instead focus on an immediate concern, is one of the easiest ways to feel like you're making progress when you're really backsliding.

For instance, when we ask an employee, "Can you get it done? What are your obstacles?" a common response we get is: "I'm too busy. I'm up to my ankles in alligators and I haven't got time to drain the swamp."—or words to that effect. When that happens, we ask them to nominate the biggest time-consuming process they're faced with during their normal working day. We then suggest doing a Fast Process Improvement for that repetitive process, aimed at reducing their personal time commitment.

This usually works a treat and triggers a "flywheel effect". By addressing their biggest time management problem, some of their valuable time is freed up to participate in further process improvement projects in the future.

During this 3-month FOUNDATION Phase, you need to get the message across to the Management Team that they must all work hard to engage the workforce in the process. It's not enough for the Management Team to be fired up and doing things in isolation from the rest of the employees. It's a case of "going all in" for transformation. And that clearly begins with you, the CEO.

Now that you appreciate the commitments required, it's time to reveal the MBE approach.

PART 2:

WHAT IS MY BUSINESS EXCELLENCE®?

My Business Excellence® is a comprehensive approach to business transformation and therefore has many components. In this Part 2, we present the key concepts. Later, in Part 3, we describe in detail how the whole thing can be implemented.

Origin of the MBE Reference Framework

The MBE Reference Framework is the product of over 30 years of evolution. The framework was originally developed to align with formulation and execution of 3-year Strategic Plans. For most businesses, we still recommend a 3-year time horizon for long-term strategy to be updated each month and formally rolled forward at each annual review. However, as today's markets and consumer preferences are changing so fast, three years can feel like an over-extended period for some businesses.

Depending on your feeling of how fast your markets are changing and the uncertainty thus created, we recommend one, two, three or five years for your rolling Strategic Plan, but always with a focus on the first year. The Intrepid Group currently uses a 5-year strategic planning timeframe because their business and markets are now relatively mature. Fourteen years ago, their planning timeframe was three years.

However, when it comes to *implementation* of the full MBE approach for it to become "business as usual", we advocate a 2-year program because it takes a minimum of two years to instill a new culture in any business.

During these two years, you will master all the "how to" basics and run process improvement projects in all areas of the business. In the third year and beyond, you and your people will consolidate their knowledge, further expand the scope of the program across the business and reap more of the compounding net benefits. During your third year, your people will simply be applying more of the same techniques mastered during your first two years. A true culture of continuous improvement should be within your grasp at that stage.

Some businesses may struggle initially and therefore take a little longer than two years to achieve the required cultural transition. Even so, this is 2-3 times faster than the serial project-by-project approach of the international frameworks for business excellence.

The key to success lies in the power and simplicity of the MBE Reference Framework that guides overall implementation.

1-page MBE Reference Framework

As mentioned earlier, there are 80 or so international frameworks for business excellence around the globe, each with their own criteria. Fortunately, there is a lot of overlap. Most of these national frameworks share the *same* 7-9 Criteria for business excellence, even though their wording may be slightly different.

For example, here are the 7 criteria of the US Baldrige Excellence Framework:

> Leadership; Strategy; Customers; Workforce; Operations; Results; Measurement, Analysis and Knowledge Management

And here are the 9 criteria of the European (EFQM) framework advocated by 34 countries:

> Leadership; Strategy; Partnerships & Resources; Processes, Products and Services; People Results; Customer Results; Society Results; Business Results

In our simplified MBE Reference Framework, we summarize all these criteria as five high-level *Prerequisites* for business excellence that are much easier for all to understand, remember, and apply.

With Customer Delight as the measuring stick and filter for success throughout, the MBE approach results in delivery of all five Prerequisites for true business excellence:

- Process Design & Improvement
- Shared Strategic Direction
- Performance Measurement & Feedback
- Knowledge Capture & Leverage
- Leadership & Management of Change

Figure 7 shows the five Prerequisites in relation to each other, all driven by the need for Customer Delight.

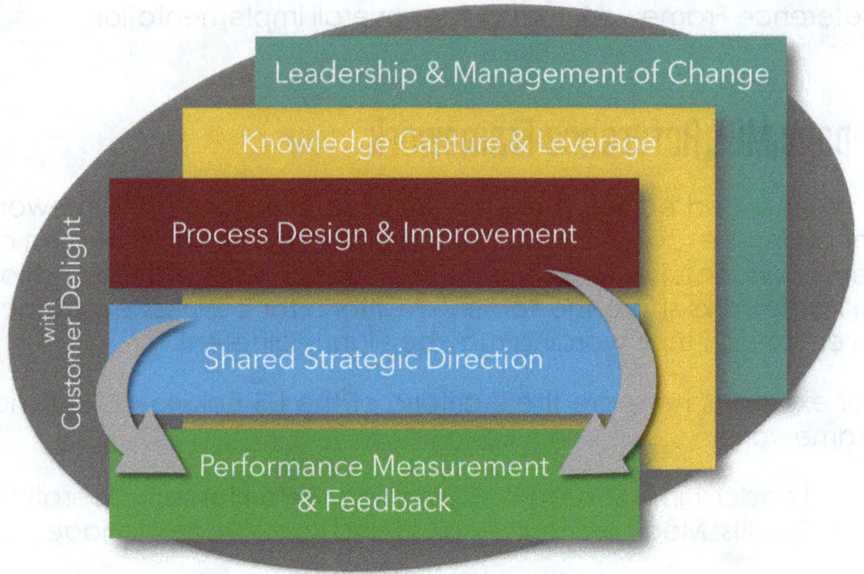

Figure 7: The MBE Reference Framework of five Prerequisites for true business excellence

The fundamental focus of all five Prerequisites is Customer Delight. In the past it was usually sufficient for a company's *product* to be better than the competition's product. Today, however, we know different. Your customer's *experience* must be better than the experience offered by the competition.

For maximum impact, all five Prerequisites must be tightly integrated during implementation. Let's look at each one in turn...

Overview of the Five Prerequisites

Process Design & Improvement

All work in a business is done through its processes.

We make extensive use of this important principle throughout the entire MBE approach to building business excellence and organizational agility.

Since all work is done through processes, and approximately 95% of all processes in business are repetitive, it follows that to dramatically improve business operations, you must improve the way you design and improve your repetitive processes.

To get started with Process Design & Improvement, the Management Team needs to agree on its repetitive Key Processes. The next step is to assign a member of the Management Team to become the willing part-time Process Manager for each one. In the case of a very small business, a Management Team member may need to assume the Process Manager role for more than one Key Process.

From then on, everything done to improve the business both operationally and strategically is linked directly to these Key Processes, with the Process Manager being fully accountable for the ongoing health and improvement of their assigned Key Process.

It is important to note that the Process Manager will be accountable irrespective of whether the assigned Key Process and associated resources are entirely within their normal line management responsibility or (more likely) are executed in part by other organizational units.

This marks the beginning of cross-functional collaboration, so critical for an organization to become truly agile. Each Process Manager's responsibilities thus become two-fold:

1. Manage their own organizational unit
2. Manage their own Key Process on behalf of the entire business

The latter will require time allocation of about a half-day per week.

DOWNTIME and Cycle Time

The aim of Process Design & Improvement is to remove all types of waste and streamline the task sequences so that the Key Processes and sub-processes perform both faster and better. Anything that doesn't increase value in the eye of the customer must be considered waste and every effort should be made to eliminate that waste. Here are the eight main types of waste and the DOWNTIME acronym for remembering them[18]...

- **D**efects
- **O**verproduction
- **W**aiting
- **N**ot utilizing talent
- **T**ransportation
- **I**nventory excess
- **M**otion waste
- **E**xcessive processing

Not all are present in every process.

Here's a simple example of waste, in this case, "Excessive processing": When you write an email, you usually have to include your contact information. Thankfully, you can simply include a signature box with all your contact information available by default with just a few seconds' effort. Imagine about how much time you're saving by using the signature box instead of repeatedly typing out your contact information in every email you send.

Sadly, most SMEs either rely on the mantra, "If it ain't broke, don't fix it," or they use band-aid solutions that are temporary and don't last. The trouble is that if a process is not efficient and effective, it *is* broken and really does need fixing permanently.

In 1939, Walter Shewhart invented today's most popular method for improving repetitive processes—the PDCA Cycle[18]. It is still the most efficient and effective method for process improvement around the globe.

Shewhart's improvement method is applicable to all repetitive processes. However, for processes that occur only once, the traditional and well-known project management method is the most appropriate for implementation. For example, you would naturally apply project management to relocate your company's Head Office to another location.

The Shewhart method involves simple team-based techniques to quickly identify and then permanently fix the so-called root causes of a process problem, thereby eliminating that problem. We will explain Shewhart's PDCA method in more detail in Part 3 of this book.

The key focus of process improvement should be Cycle Time Reduction. You may be familiar with this concept under the term "Lean Thinking" as championed by Toyota and others in the pursuit of excellence.

Cycle Time is defined as the average *calendar* time required to execute any repetitive process, while matching or exceeding the customer's expectations. It is measured in *calendar* time (not work time) because calendar time is what customers care about. They are not interested in how much work time is required to complete a product or task.

The world's manufacturers have long since recognized that minimal Cycle Time is critical in manufacturing—hence "Just-In-Time" (JIT) programs first implemented some 70 years ago.

Several decades later, the world's leading service sector businesses realized the same was true of their endeavors. About 50-85% of service sector business costs are for salaries and benefits which purchase employee work time so that the organization has the means to execute its processes.

By removing process waste, the efforts of employees can be devoted to the value-adding process steps. The business does more with less effort.

The benefits of controlling process Cycle Time become clear once we realize that poor processes waste time in one form or another, and this squanders a service organization's resources through the inefficient use of employee effort.

Whether you have a manufacturing or service business, minimizing the Cycle Times of your company's key processes will enable time at work (for employees or machinery) to be used to its maximum effect. Figure 8 shows some of the many adverse contributors to overall Cycle Time that need to be targeted in process improvement projects...

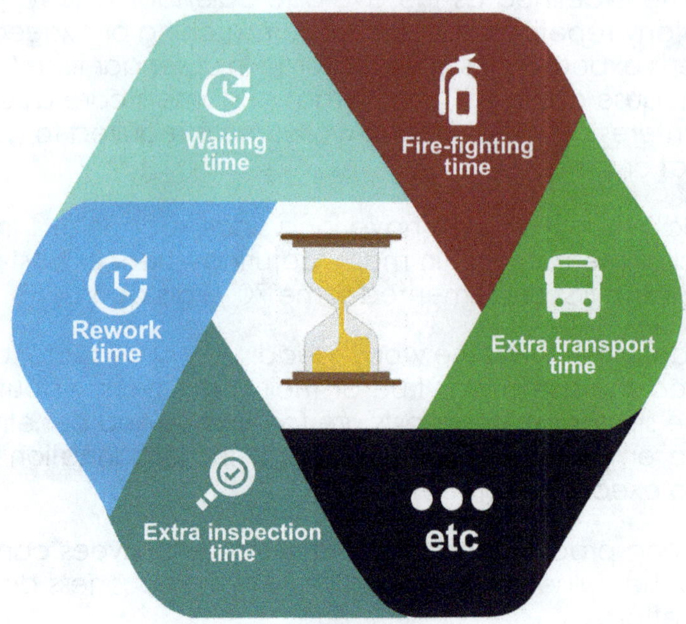

Figure 8: Adverse contributors to overall Cycle Time

From the 1960s to the 1990s, the Westinghouse Corporation developed a technique known as Cost-Time Profiling[19,20]. This technique quantifies the combined time and cost impacts of process improvements. As they say in the classics: "Time is Money", as illustrated in Figure 9.

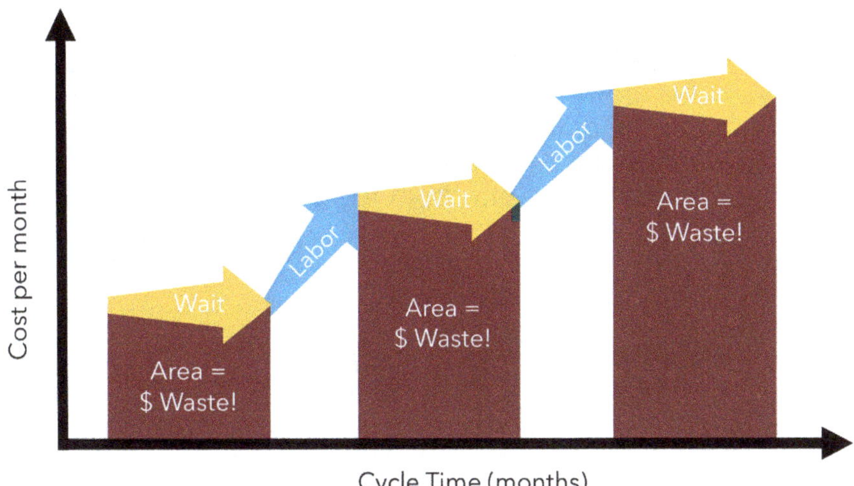

Figure 9: Cost-Time Profiling highlights the wasted cost of wait times during process hand-offs (i.e., the areas beneath each wait time)

You may find it startling to learn that as a result of many Cost-Time Profiling projects conducted by the Westinghouse Corporation over 50 years, they reduced Cycle Times in their service businesses by an average of 50%, and their costs automatically reduced by an average of 10-15%[19]. This is what you want to see happen in your business. These days, even manufacturers have a substantial service business dimension.

It's even more exciting to realize that reducing overall Cycle Time by 50% in a service business is *easy* to do because we know that, on average, about 95% of the total Cycle Time is consumed by employees either waiting or handing off their work to the next employee or team.

Think about it. Typically, 95% of the total Cycle Time of processes in your service business is wasted and creates no customer value.

Focusing on reducing Cycle Time is a quick way to add customer value and either decrease costs or apply any released resources to other aspects of the company's production. This adds to the company's profit margin and improves its capability to beat the competition. This is simple, exciting stuff. And it doesn't take much to turn you into the shareholders' hero.

You would have to agree this is a far easier way of reducing costs compared to cutting the budget by 10-15% or reducing employee head count by the same 10-15% which, by the way, does zip for improving the company's processes. Employees should never be laid off as a result of their participation in process improvement projects. To do so would immediately put a stop to further voluntary process improvement efforts. In fact, a good selling point to institutionalizing process improvement is to inform employees that it helps secure their jobs, and the increased business performance may even result in salary raises or bonuses.

Cycle Time reduction is a win for all parties. The customer wins since they get the right product or service faster. The business wins because it produces the product or service at a lower cost, which either translates into higher margins or increased productivity. The employees win because they retain their jobs and no longer have to deal with frustrating and outdated processes which negatively impact their work-life balance—and might even receive a bonus if you so wish.

Everybody wins when Cycle Time is reduced. When everybody wins, YOU win.

The misuse of employee time results in the opposite: lose-lose-lose. The customer loses because they have to wait to get what they want. The business loses because lost time incurs unnecessary employee wage costs, and this reduces the profit margin. The employees lose because they have to deal with the frustrations of inefficiency in their jobs and working hard over long hours for poor results.

The quality award-winning US-based Xerox organization arguably said it best many years ago: "Process hand-offs kill you in business."

It's important to note here that Cycle Time is heavily influenced by your organizational structure.

Figure 10 illustrates the Cycle Time problem with classic functional organizational structures in larger SMEs that have multiple specialist groups (e.g., Marketing; Finance; Civil Design; Mechanical Design; Electrical Design; Estimating; Construction; Maintenance).

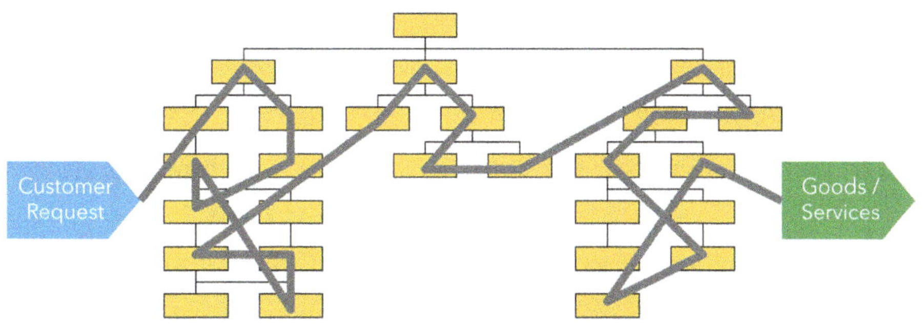

Time gets lost in the "white space" between organisational units and layers. Reminder: Today's customers want "the right stuff FAST"!

Figure 10: The "hand-off" problem with organization structures that have lots of specialty units and multiple reporting layers

As you can see, an excessive number of vertical and horizontal "hand-offs" will have a dramatic negative impact on overall Cycle Time for the customer. This is the main reason why world-class organizations are consciously structured to be "flat." How flat is your organization?

If your SME organization does have multiple specialist units, you should consider reorganizing the structure along process lines such that all the employees involved in executing any Key Process will report to the one Process Manager.

Deep, functional organization structures can also limit the organization's ability to deploy strategy effectively to lower levels of the business, particularly if the functional units act as separate "silos".

Irrespective of the organizational structure, the best way to break down silo barriers is to make extensive use of small and autonomous cross-functional teams undertaking a steady stream of quarterly Projects aligned to the strategic Objectives.

Shared Strategic Direction

Having a shared strategic direction is essential so that everyone can "pull the rope in the same direction". An SME, or any organization for that matter, cannot be fully productive and may not even survive if individuals or groups within the organization have conflicting goals and contrary directions. Everyone must contribute to business productivity, or the business can only advance slowly, if at all.

This is common sense. It's also why many managers, following a company takeover, will "clean house" and put their own people in place because they know they can count on their loyalty and willingness to follow instructions.

Understanding where your business is NOW, WHERE you wish to go over the planning period (typically one, two, three or five years), and HOW you plan to get there are three crucial considerations in developing a shared strategic direction for the business.

Figure 11 shows how your strategic Objectives can be progressively deployed through quarterly process improvement Projects.

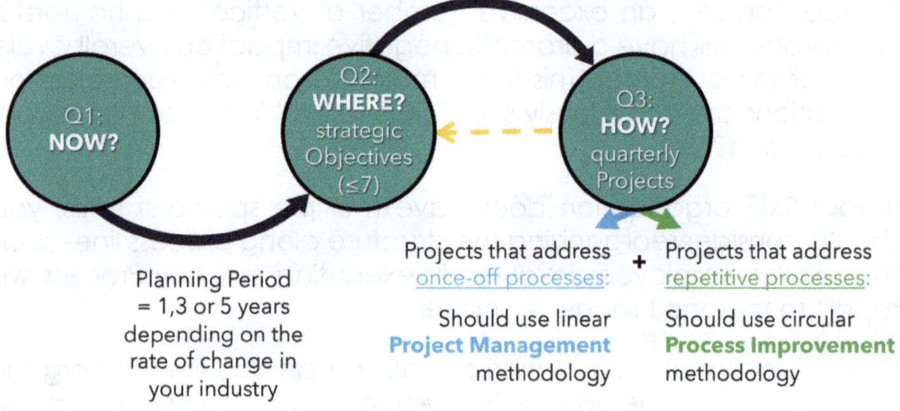
Q1:
NOW?
Q2:
WHERE?
strategic
Objectives
(≤7)
Q3:
HOW?
quarterly
Projects
Planning Period
= 1,3 or 5 years
depending on the
rate of change in
your industry
Projects that address
once-off processes:
Should use linear
Project Management
methodology
+
Projects that address
repetitive processes:
Should use circular
Process Improvement
methodology

Figure 11: Formulating your Strategic Plan by addressing three big questions in order and then deploying the Objectives through regular quarterly Projects of two types

A sound strategy developed this way creates realistic expectations, because everyone understands the way forward. The strategy includes a clear and long-term VISION of what the company is trying to achieve (i.e., its Winning Aspiration) plus Objectives that need to be delivered by the end of the chosen planning period (i.e., one, three, or five years out). Quarterly Projects are required to progressively deliver each Objective.

When the Strategic Plan is formulated, you will go through a simple but powerful way of ensuring that the highest potential risks in pursuing each strategic Objective are properly managed. Provided the resultant risk-managed strategy is shared with everyone, top-to-bottom business alignment and workforce empowerment can follow.

The good news is that mastery of this Prerequisite *amplifies* the success of the other four Prerequisites of the MBE Reference Framework. What a great deal.

Performance Measurement & Feedback

Three well-known adages highlight the importance of measurement and feedback when undertaking business improvement:

1. *"We are what we measure."*
2. *"What gets measured, gets managed."*
3. *"If you can't measure it, you can't improve it."*

It's impossible to improve something if you don't first understand the nature of the problem and see the issues clearly. Measurement creates visibility and leads to understanding. Measurement and feedback enable corrective action to be taken to improve an emerging negative situation.

This is why mastery of Performance Measurement & Feedback is crucial for business improvement.

Measurement for its own sake is meaningless. The challenge is to find the right measures for your business. As shown in Figure 12, the MBE Reference Framework mandates only two essential categories of high-level Key Performance Indicators (KPIs) for your business:

1. **KPIs that regularly monitor the Operational health of your business.** These KPIs are found by first identifying and agreeing all the Key Processes of your business, and for each then answering the question: "What MUST we measure over the immediate 12-month period to ensure that this Key Process is trending in a positive, healthy manner?"

2. **KPIs that regularly monitor the Strategic health of your business.** These KPIs are identified after your Management Team formulates the strategic Objectives for the planning period, and for each then answering the question: "What MUST we measure over the immediate 12-month period to convince ourselves that we are progressively achieving this Objective?"

Reminder: There are no other high level KPIs for your business!

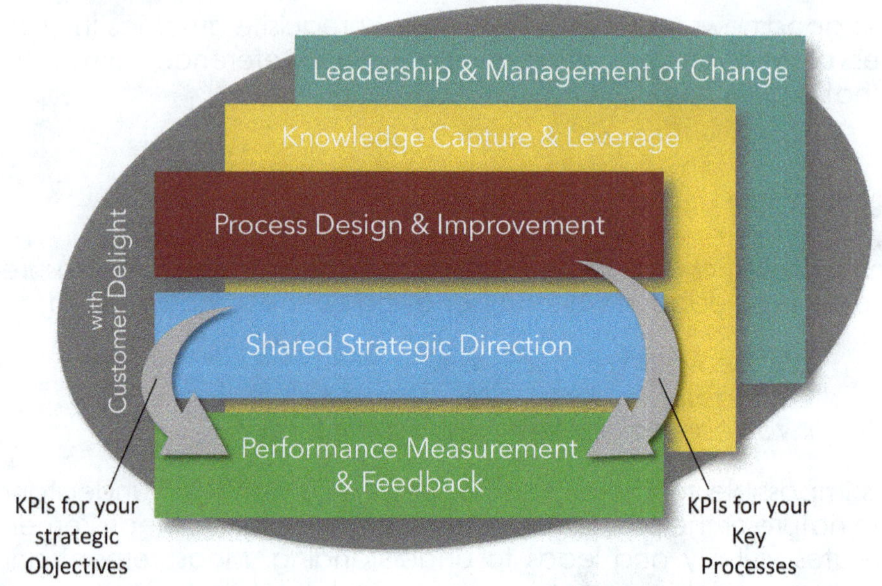

Figure 12: There are only two categories of high level KPIs for your business

When specifying high level KPIs, you should limit the total number to only those that result from the above sequence. Should you decide to track more than only the most important ones, you will burden your Management Team with unnecessary effort, cost, and lost time.

As we'll discuss in Part 3, the tracking of all KPIs, not just these high-level ones, should be automated in graphical form so that the results are available on demand to all concerned, and emerging trends are visually evident.

Knowledge Capture & Leverage

It's no secret that we all live in a knowledge economy—an economy in which growth is dependent on the quantity, quality, and accessibility of the information available, rather than the means of production.

Knowledge Capture & Leverage has become increasingly important for businesses over the past 60 years as organizational assets continue to become more knowledge-based and less finance-based.

There are three main reasons why Knowledge Capture & Leverage is a Prerequisite for every world class business...

1. The advent of IT technology and the Internet have accelerated our ability to capture and share knowledge easily and at great speed.

2. Globalization has made it imperative that the business is aware of progress and competition in other countries—to guard against disruption and to capitalize on new market opportunities.

3. The workforce of today has become highly mobile, and when an employee leaves the business, they take their knowledge with them unless management finds a way to capture it beforehand.

This Prerequisite is intimately linked to Process Design & Improvement. Since all work is done through processes, your organization's best practices for process execution plus any critical associated knowledge should be captured and made readily available via suitable support software for authorized employee access. When an employee needs to know how best to do their job, the latest knowledge should be available to them on demand and at an appropriate level of detail.

As shown in our MBE Reference Framework (i.e., Figures 7,12), knowledge also needs to be captured and leveraged in Shared Strategic Direction and in Performance Measurement & Feedback.

This is why Knowledge Capture & Leverage is depicted as "overlaying" these other three Prerequisites. The intent is to capture the organization's collective expertise wherever it resides—on paper, in databases or in your employees' minds—and distribute it to wherever the information can be used to greatest effect.

There are two fundamental ways to do this, and our MBE approach incorporates both:

1. **The Codification Approach (or "people-to-documents" approach)** in which knowledge is collected, codified, and shared with the help of IT. Since all work is done through processes, it makes sense to capture and store knowledge according to

which Key Process is under consideration. It also makes sense to link that knowledge directly to the individual steps and sub-steps of that Key Process. This enables easy graphical portrayal of knowledge via the organization's process hierarchy.

The combined process and knowledge flows are stored in the organization's digital Quality Management System (QMS).

A QMS is a collection of documented business processes focused on consistently meeting or exceeding customer requirements and enhancing their satisfaction[21]. The QMS is aligned with the organization's role and strategic direction. Included in the QMS are the organization's vision and Objectives, policies, documented information, and resources needed to implement and maintain it.

Crucially, your QMS should also contain readily accessible guidance for employees down to the required level of detail on the "best known way" of executing every Key Process of the business. It is maintained by adding or updating the relevant content after every process improvement activity.

Your QMS cannot be developed overnight. It will need to be progressively developed over years and should never be finished. The responsibilities for managers and employees in building and maintaining the QMS need to be clear. Other success factors include having the right IT support tools and a process for building the QMS methodically.

If desired, you may obtain certification of your operational QMS against the international QMS Standard, currently ISO 9001:2015[22]. By following our overall MBE approach to business excellence, certification can be achieved with little additional effort because all the basics will be in place.

2. **The Personalization Approach (or "people-to-people" approach)** in which people are linked so that knowledge of how to do things the best way can be shared in person. The focus here is on dialogue between individuals.

   This human interaction method is carried out in the MBE approach by using teams to share information at critical junctures throughout the implementation, such as:

- When deploying strategic Objectives via quarterly Fast Process Improvement (FPI) Projects and Standard Projects
- When formulating and updating the Strategic Plan
- When reviewing business performance each month and year
- When undertaking large Business Process Reengineering (BPR) Projects

All this ensures that peoples' views are acknowledged about what is currently being done, and what needs to be changed.

For instance, our standard 2-day BPR Planning Workshop, explained in detail later, begins with participants of the targeted Key Process sharing their views on what problems currently exist. Later in the Workshop, the participants work collaboratively to design the new "best practice" way of executing the process. In so doing, they ensure that all the identified weaknesses of the current process are eliminated. The overall BPR process ensures knowledge sharing and buy-in by all concerned.

Leadership & Management of Change

Many industry commentators have observed that the only constant for a modern business is change. Your journey of becoming a high performing business will involve momentous change as you develop a culture of continuous improvement and shared knowledge.

Leadership and Management are different, yet both are essential for high performance:

- **Leadership is *emotional*—it deals with the emotions of change.** Leadership encompasses emotional concepts like the organization's long-term Vision, its set of agreed values and behaviors, its work culture, shared strategic direction, employee engagement, diversity, and business ethics.
- **Management is *clinical*—it deals with the complexities of change.** We manage cash, we manage processes, we manage problem-solving and we manage the annual budget.

A balance of the two is required. Brilliant Leadership without Management leads to employees who are excited about the business but unable to execute effectively. On the other hand, brilliant Management without Leadership leads to sound plans ready for execution but no passionate employees to push those plans forward. Your best people would likely leave for more exciting roles elsewhere.

The absence of top-level leadership buy-in for change is widely regarded as one major cause of failure in business transformation programs across the globe[23]. Without top level buy-in, there are no role models, no commitment to a long-term program of constant change, and inadequate resourcing. Enjoying the benefits of a culture founded on continuous improvement, with openly shared knowledge between empowered employees, would remain a pipe dream.

As indicated in our MBE Reference Framework, this Prerequisite overlays all four of the other Prerequisites simply because Leadership & Management of Change cannot be implemented successfully in isolation from the activities of the other four Prerequisites.

To continuously improve the business, change must become a welcome constant. As leaders, we must be proactive in leading and managing change at all levels of the organization. Because of this, the collective impact of the Leadership Styles of individual managers (Figure 6) must be given considerable attention when building a world class business.

1-page Integration Blueprint for Business Excellence

As a result of facilitating excellence in SMEs over the past 30 years via the high-level MBE Reference Framework, we have developed a unique blueprint which ties together all the core components of both operational excellence and strategic excellence in a way that encourages business agility.

The MBE Integration Blueprint shown in Figure 13 does three things...

1. Identifies each component required for Operational excellence
2. Identifies each component required for Strategic excellence

3. Places every component adjacent to the other components that must be integrated seamlessly with it to avoid losses and unnecessary waste

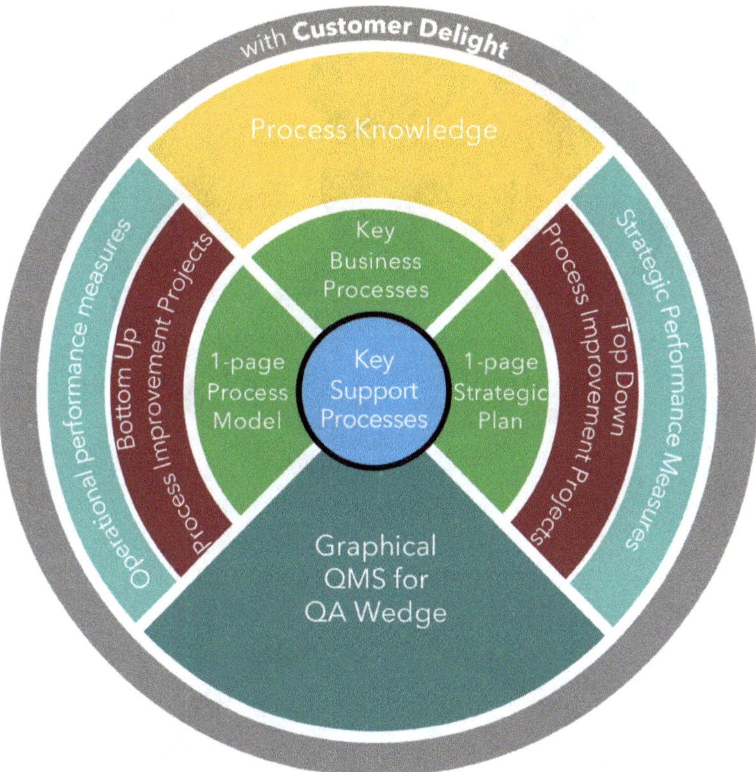

Figure 13: The 1-page MBE Integration Blueprint for Business Excellence

As shown in Figure 14, this integration for full business excellence may be regarded as one blueprint for Operational excellence plus another for Strategic excellence.

OPERATIONAL Excellence

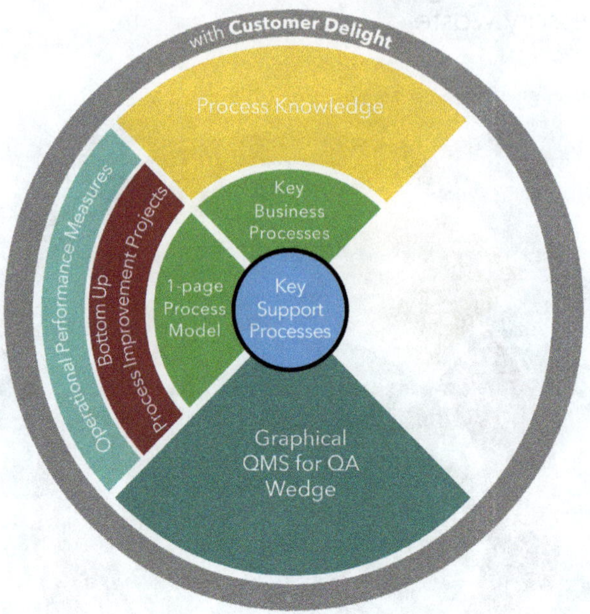

STRATEGIC Excellence

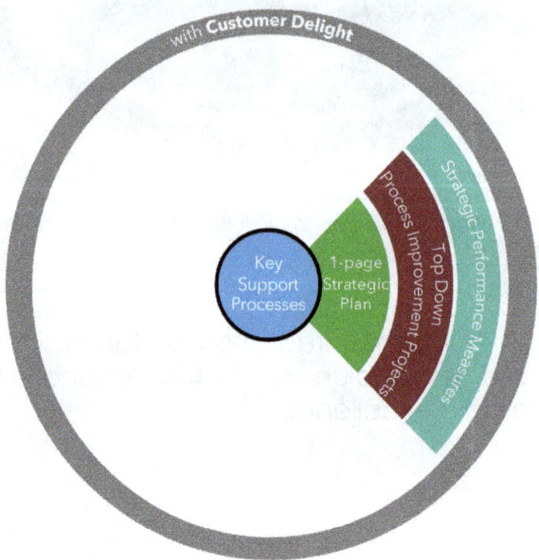

Figure 14: Integration Blueprints for Operational Excellence and Strategic Excellence

These blueprints indicate how everything needs to be interlinked for maximum impact. The MBE team continues to apply them in designing and building the tools to support pragmatic implementation of the entire MBE approach.

The two most important elements mentioned in Figure 14 are the 1-page Process Model and the 1-page Strategic Plan. To be memorable, both need to be represented in graphical form.

- The 1-page Process Model shows the current Role of the business plus all its key repetitive processes.
- The 1-page Strategic Plan shows the long-term Vision for the business plus all its strategic Objectives for the chosen planning period (i.e., usually one, two, or three years).

Both the 1-page Process Model and the 1-page Strategic Plan are developed by the Management Team during the 2-day Foundation Planning Workshop that will mark the beginning of your journey towards full business excellence.

Power of Graphical Imagery

The power of having and using graphical diagrams and models should not be underestimated. Condensing your operational processes, strategic Objectives, project briefs, net benefits, and other major business excellence improvement components onto single pages has the dual advantages of allowing you and your people to see the big picture and think clearly about priorities.

There are two graphical images that do the heavy lifting for the overall MBE approach:

The 1-page Process Model, which drives all your Operational excellence initiatives

- The 1-page Strategic Plan, which drives all your Strategic excellence initiatives

1-page Process Model

We start consideration of your 1-page Process Model with an important definition:

Process Definition

As shown in Figure 15, a "process" is a sequence of activities that converts inputs into outputs for a customer (internal or external). The process may occur only once, or it may be repetitive.

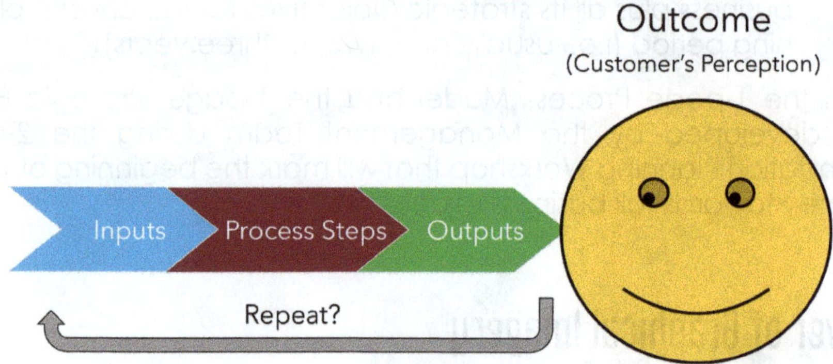

Figure 15: Definition of a Process

Process Thinking

Process thinking is central to Operational excellence and the 1-page Process Model that drives it. Process thinking may be summarized as follows:

- All work is done through processes.
- To improve operations, the processes must be improved.
- Repetitive processes are far more prevalent in business than once-only processes
- Improving a repetitive process requires a different technique to the one for improving a once-only process.
- Being proactive and targeting processes for improvement will deliver far better outcomes than simply reacting to process problems when they occur.

- A proactive approach to targeting processes for improvement is much easier and more effective after the business has reached agreement on what its Key Processes are.

Some existing processes may be well-designed while others are poorly designed. Some may be well-documented and others poorly documented. Irrespective of how they may be described, your business is already executing thousands of repetitive processes every day. These range from the very small (e.g., Answer the phone) to the very large (e.g., Do the job).

If you want your business to be high performing, you must target your most important processes. Your business cannot begin designing and improving its Key Processes until you and your Management Team first identify what they are. Sooner rather than later, these Key Processes will need to be designed properly and then continually improved to be as efficient and effective as possible.

Proactive Process Design & Improvement is therefore a critical competency for any organization aspiring to perform at its highest levels. This is why it is one of the five Prerequisites for business excellence. Unfortunately, most SMEs are passive and accept what comes. They miss out on the massive net benefits that flow from a well-structured approach to Process Design & Improvement. Don't let this happen to your business.

All Your Key Processes on a Single Page

Today, you have the benefit of learning from thousands of high-performing businesses around the world that have already been down this path. They found it is much easier to understand how to design and improve processes if the key repetitive processes that deliver products or services to external customers are separated from the key repetitive processes that service the internal customers (i.e., your own employees).

Our MBE approach has a tool that does exactly this. The 1-page Process Model shows all your key repetitive processes on a single page. Figure 16 shows an example for a steel fabrication business:

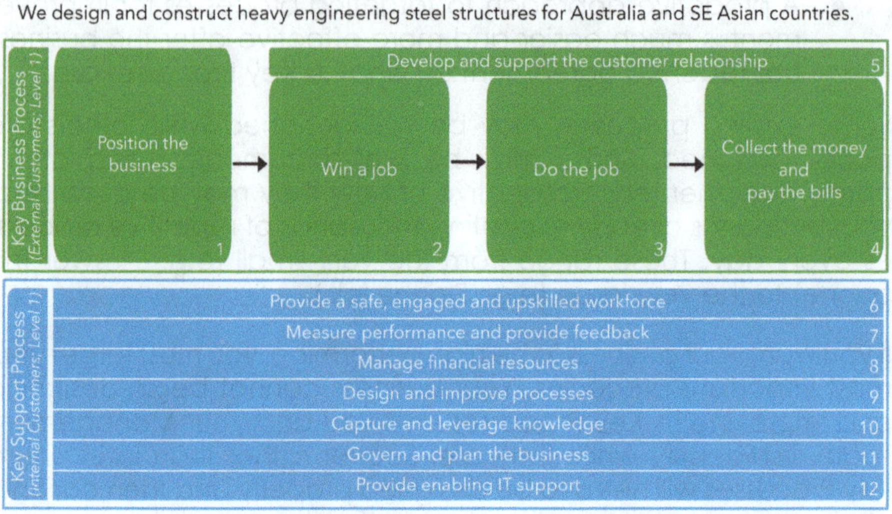

We design and construct heavy engineering steel structures for Australia and SE Asian countries.

Key Business Process
(External Customers; Level 1)

Develop and support the customer relationship 5

Position the business 1 → Win a job 2 → Do the job 3 → Collect the money and pay the bills 4

Key Support Process
(Internal Customers; Level 1)

Provide a safe, engaged and upskilled workforce 6
Measure performance and provide feedback 7
Manage financial resources 8
Design and improve processes 9
Capture and leverage knowledge 10
Govern and plan the business 11
Provide enabling IT support 12

Figure 16: Example of a 1-page Process Model

Note: The 1-page Process Model depicts only the repetitive key processes of the business, not the occasional process that occurs only once (e.g., Launch the business on the stock exchange). Six Sigma research informs us that approximately 95% of all processes in business are repetitive and only 5% occur just once. As we shall see in Part 3, these statistics have big implications on how process improvements should be realized.

Single-Sentence ROLE Statement

The ROLE statement at the top should summarize, in clinical terms, what the business will be doing for the chosen planning period. It should be devoid of emotion and should be a single, short sentence that begins with the word "We..." and finishes with a full stop. In between there should be three components of the sentence:

- First, there are up to three value-adding words. In the above example they are "design" and "construct". Any more than three such words would make the sentence difficult to remember.
- Second, there are a few words that summarize your full set of offerings. In the above example, they are "heavy engineering steel structures".

- Third, there are words that summarize your target market(s). In the above example, they are "Australia and SE Asian countries". The markets do not need to be geographical. For example, "for people with dental problems."

Combining all 3 elements we get the complete ROLE statement: "We design and construct heavy engineering steel structures for Australia and SE Asian countries".

Your ROLE statement effectively describes the "meta" process for your business (i.e., what it does, day in and day out). Because the wording is clinical, i.e., devoid of any emotion whatsoever, it is a management concept not a leadership concept. The emotion comes in later when you formulate your company's long-term VISION statement that will drive your 1-page Strategic Plan.

When someone currently asks you, "What does your business do?" does your response make it easy for them to understand, or is the person performing mental gymnastics trying to understand your 2-minute response? The more effort it takes for someone to understand what you do, the less likely it is that person will regard you as someone who can help them with a problem. And even if they aren't a potential customer, they might talk to someone who is.

In the MBE approach to excellence, the ROLE statement enables you and all your people to articulate clearly what your business does in a single, memorable sentence. As the CEO, you should strongly encourage all your people to learn this single sentence off by heart. You may choose to display it prominently on your website and in any printed marketing material.

Using your 1-page Process Model

Below the ROLE statement, the 1-page Process Model depicts all your Key Business Processes in green and all your internal Key Support Processes in blue. As shown in Figure 16, the Key Business Processes are for your external customers and the Key Support Processes are for your internal customers (i.e., your own employees).

By representing all your Key Processes this way, your employees can understand and benefit from a shared view of the entire business operation. For example, when an employee reflects on which Key Process(es) they are involved in, they quickly realize that their own job lies somewhere on this page. This is critical information when reviewing individual job performance, setting new commitments, and creating Personal Development Plans (PDPs) for the next employee review period.

Importantly, once this 1-page Process Model has been developed and agreed by your Management Team, it provides a focus for all process improvement activities within your business. Occasionally, a Key Process will be targeted for top-down improvement, and frequently, sub-processes (i.e., smaller parts of the same process) will be targeted for bottom-up improvement.

Accountability for Process Managers

When everyone is accountable, no-one is accountable. Remember our story about Everybody, Somebody, Anybody, and Nobody? Here's another one, about the same four characters and change:

> *Once there were four people named Everybody, Somebody, Anybody, Nobody who wanted change.*
>
> *Everybody said, "I want change."*
>
> *Somebody said, "If only Anybody would start to change, I would, too."*
>
> *Nobody said, "I will change."*
>
> *Finally, Everybody stayed the same, blaming Somebody for waiting for Anybody to start changing. Nobody changed.*

By marking your 1-page Process Model with the initials of each designated Process Manager, as shown in Figure 17, and then disseminating the page throughout the entire organization, everyone will know who is accountable for the performance of each Key Process within your business.

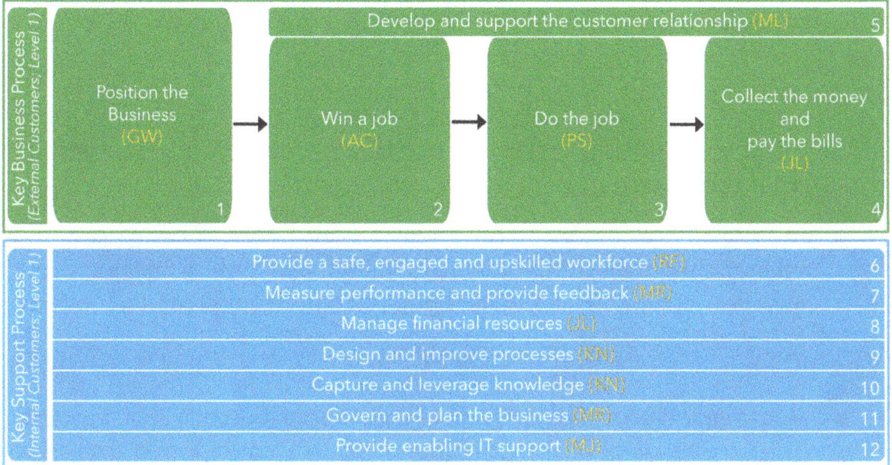

Figure 17: Example of a 1-page Process Model with assigned Process Managers (in brackets)

Each Process Manager's responsibility is cross-functional and so applies across all organizational unit boundaries.

The Process Manager has the responsibility for making continual improvements to their assigned Key Process(es). This must be considered an integral part of their job going forward. To make room for this new responsibility, they may need to delegate some of their line management responsibilities to their direct report staff. It should be unacceptable for them to argue, "Sorry, but I am too busy." In this regard, the Management Team is only as good as its weakest link.

Because the Process Manager will be held accountable by the Management Team for their process performance, they will be vitally interested in setting and monitoring the KPI(s) that track the health status of their own assigned Key Process(es).

The role of every Process Manager includes the following:

- Be the senior person in the organization responsible for the design and improvement of the assigned end-to-end Key Process(es,) irrespective of who "owns" the employees in the current organizational structure
- Champion continuous process improvement with support from the CEO

- Select one (or maybe more) KPI for determining the operational health of the process, and monitor the KPI trend every month
- Sponsor process improvement projects to address perceived process under-performance, and to deploy strategic Objectives that place added demands on the assigned Key Process(es)
- As part of every process improvement project, ensure that adequate Quality Assurance (QA) is in place to guarantee on-going exemplary execution of the improved Key Process.

Accountability for each Process Manager is ensured by having:

- A clearly defined role that encompasses both line management responsibilities and the above process management responsibilities;
- A maximum of three assigned Key Processes, to maintain focus and avoid personal overload in sponsoring process improvements;
- Their own chosen KPI(s) to gauge performance of the assigned Key Process(es) at the monthly Progress Review Meeting of the Management Team;
- An organization-wide, digitally-based Quality Management System (QMS) that guarantees proper on-going execution of their assigned Key Process(es) via the four standard QA requirements (i.e., Document; Train; Measure; Celebrate).

Process Reengineering Priorities

If occasional, top-down reengineering of your Key Business Processes from end to end is not done well, your business performance will always be sub-optimal.

Your Business Process Reengineering (BPR) Project priorities and their proposed timings over the strategic planning period should be indicated clearly on your 1-page Process Model. Continuing with our construction company example, you can see in Figure 18 how the BPR Project priorities and their timing over the Management Team's chosen planning period (in this case three years) are highlighted.

We design and construct heavy engineering steel structures for Australia and SE Asian countries.

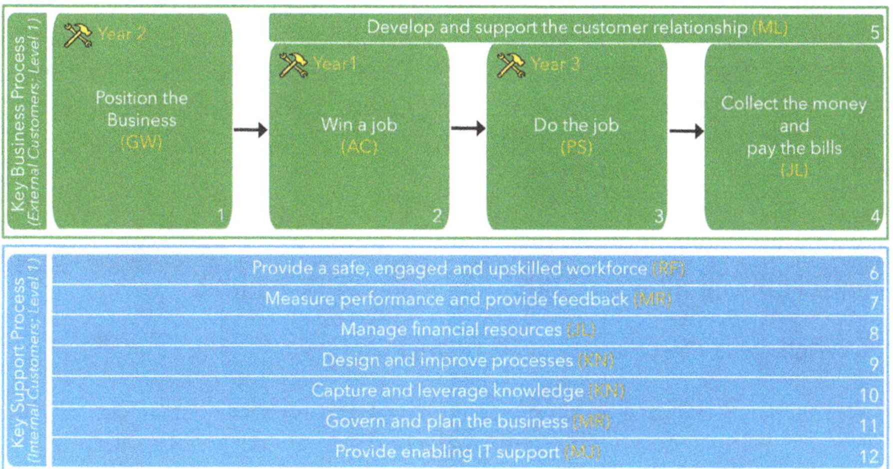

Figure 18: Example of a 1-page Process Model with agreed BPR Project priorities and their proposed timing

Due to the significant added pressures on staff and financial resources, only one or two BPR Projects should be undertaken each year. This minimizes the change management challenges, while ensuring that no Key Business Process ever gets more than about seven years out of date. If only one green Key Business Process is reengineered every year as shown in the example of Figure 18, this target would be met easily because all the Key Business Processes would be reengineered within just five years.

Your prioritized BPR Projects should be carried forward explicitly into your 1-page Strategic Plan (see following) because, by their very nature, they will have strategic impact on the future of your business.

<u>Note</u>: There is no need to reengineer any of the Key *Support* Processes, because reengineered versions of these are shared openly on the Internet. These seven blue processes are common to every business, and so there is little industry hesitation in sharing reengineered versions. One such popular source is the website: www.apqc.org.

Reengineered green Key *Business* Processes, however, are rarely shared because they embody each organization's competitive positioning in the marketplace. This is why your business needs to do its own reengineering for these.

Further Examples of 1-page Process Models

Several examples of 1-page Process Models for different business types are presented in Appendix B. Feel free to adapt one of these examples when drafting your own tailored version for your business in collaboration with your Management Team. Alternatively, you might prefer to start from scratch.

Monitoring the Health of your Key Processes via KPIs

What gets measured, gets managed

A common challenge for SMEs is how best to identify and measure the *right* things. Most businesses do not have a rigorous and logical approach for identifying what *must* be measured to monitor the health and progress of their entire day-to-day business operation.

As you might expect, common behavior is to measure what is easy rather than what is right and in the best interest of the organization.

In implementing the MBE approach, the idea is to identify the *minimum* number of the right Key Process KPIs for RUNNING the business. Therefore, for each Key Business Process and Key Support Process in your 1-page Process Model, the designated Process Manager should specify one or more KPIs that will convince the full Management Team that the assigned Key Process is performing well.

Ideally, only *one* KPI should be chosen for each Key Process. Why incur the additional overhead of having and tracking two or more KPIs when one may be enough to convince everybody that the process is working well?

Figure 19 shows the recommended 1-page format for the complete set of Key Process KPIs. Since the seven Key Support Processes are common for all businesses, we provide some suggested KPIs that are often used to measure their operational health. These KPIs are by no means mandatory, but are often utilized by our clients.

Key Business Process	Measure (#; $; %; Nil)	Frequency (M;Q;B-A;Y)	Baseline End Last FY	Target End Current FY
1. ?	?	?	?	?
2. ?	?	?	?	?
3. ?	?	?	?	?
4. ?	?	?	?	?
5. ?	?	?	?	?

Key Support Process	Measure (#; $; %; Nil)	Frequency (M;Q;B-A;Y)	Baseline End Last FY	Target End Current FY
6. Provide a safe, engaged and upskilled workforce	% Employees who left the business (rolling past 12 months)	M	?	?
7. Measure performance and provide feedback	# Average participant meeting effectiveness rating for monthly Progress Review Meeting (1 is bad, 10 is great)	M	?	?
8. Manage financial resources	$ Net Profit (EBIT) per Employee (rolling past 12 months)	M	?	?
9. Design and improve processes	# FPI Projects completed (ytd) # BPR Projects completed per annum	M Y	?	?
10. Capture and leverage knowledge	% Employees who accessed the Process Catalogue last month	M	?	?
11. Govern and plan the business	% Quarterly Projects completed successfully	Q	?	?
12. Provide enabling IT support	% Employees who responded positively to the question "Do you have the right IT support to do your job brilliantly?"	Y	?	?

Figure 19: All KPIs for your Key Processes will be in this Table.

Rows would be added as necessary to match the number of Key Business (green) Processes of your 1-page Process Model.

Specifying each KPI ready for reporting does require attention to detail. Here are the elements you should consider:

1. Clarity over which Key Process in the 1-page Process Model is being measured
2. Precise wording so that there is zero ambiguity for how it will be quantified each reporting period
3. Type of the measurement (#; $; %; Nil)
4. Measurement Frequency (Monthly; Quarterly; Bi-Annually; Yearly)

5. Baseline—the actual value of the measure at the start of the reporting time-frame (usually the start of the Financial Year or Calendar Year)

6. Target; the forecast value of the measure at the end of the reporting time-frame (usually the end of the Financial Year or Calendar Year)

Baselines and Targets are crucial elements to provide instant visual comparison of where the business starts and what the target is for the end of the reporting time-frame. The MBE recommendation is for the reporting time-frame to be 12 months for Key Processes.

Because a fundamental element of the MBE approach is improvement, setting a target that is beyond current performance, but can be achieved by process improvement projects throughout the year, is important.

Things to consider when choosing your KPIs

When choosing your KPIs the availability of the input data should be considered. If the input data is too difficult to source, it may be wise to modify the KPI accordingly.

For example, for the Key Business Process: 'Position the Business', you may be tempted to suggest that Market Share is the obvious answer to the above question. However, obtaining reliable Market Share data on a monthly basis is likely to be far too costly if regular external market surveys were to be commissioned.

An alternative KPI such as Annual Revenue is a reasonable and much more cost-effective alternative. This information is readily available to the Process Manager for tracking. If the Annual Revenue is rising, it is reasonable to assume that the business is being well positioned in the marketplace.

It may be tempting to choose a KPI such as 'Total Monthly Revenue' instead, especially as you will be reviewing the KPI every month. However, the risk here is that monthly revenue could be significantly impacted by seasonal or cyclical factors. One way of addressing these wild swings is to "smooth" the measurement over a full year by choosing a rolling 12 month average. Each measurement would then include all 4 seasons! This KPI would now read 'Total Revenue over the immediate past 12 months, measured monthly'.

The health of a process is usually assessed in relation to the process outcome. For example for the Key Business Process: 'Invoice the Customer and collect the revenue', the desired outcome is the timely collection of money from Customers. Therefore, a KPI that measures whether or not this is happening would be an effective measure of the process health. In this instance, the KPI could be: 'Average Debtor Days outstanding at month's end'.

1-page Strategic Plan

Change is the only constant in the 21st century. Nothing ever stays the same, and you may need to take advantage of a major market opportunity or respond to a major business risk.

Here's the good news. You already know how to build a solid foundation for RUNNING your business with the techniques described for creating your 1-page Process Model and using it to target top-down and bottom-up process improvements.

As we shall see, CHANGING your business strategically is made easier because several of the very same process-related techniques apply for strategy deployment down and across the organization.

Whether your current business strategy is explicit or implicit, there is no doubt you already have one. However, you will be far more effective in changing your business for the better if you have an *explicit* strategy that you share openly with your employees. Once your employees understand and buy-into the resultant strategic Objectives, it is easy to deploy them down and across the organization through quarterly Projects implemented by small, autonomous teams.

You begin by developing your rolling Strategic Plan on one page. Why one page? Because this makes it easy to keep the Strategic Plan current during monthly and annual reviews undertaken by the Management Team.

Every business benefits from having a "stretch" view of what it would like to achieve over its chosen planning period. The planning period should be consistent with the perceived rate of change in market conditions and customer preferences. For most established businesses, one year is too short to bring about substantial strategic change. Five years is too distant for many businesses to envisage market conditions and customer trends with much confidence. Most companies adopt a 3-year timeframe for their strategic planning horizon. Very few choose two years.

Software development companies and other online, high-tech, or fast-moving industries may choose to work on a shorter timeframe, as the following case study illustrates.

Case Study—The right planning timeframe?

We once had a client that supplied software for the global gaming industry.

When they came to us for help, the company was three years old. It had grown from just the founders to about 80 employees. They had been growing exceptionally fast over the immediate past 12 months.

From the founding of the business, the company had hit the ground running without any premeditated strategic direction. Rather, they had been experimenting with their proprietary technology to see what they could do with it. This was fine when there were only a few people playing with some new toys. But quite suddenly they had an 80-strong workforce looking to the founders for direction. A number of employees had already left because they couldn't cope with the career insecurity and job stress that came with this situation.

We facilitated a 2-day Foundation Planning Workshop to chart the future of their business over the next three years. This was as much about creating alignment between the founders and the rest of the Management Team as anything else. There was a huge emotional release as a result. Now everyone knew where the company was heading.

We also trained the entire workforce on fast process improvement techniques via brief training sessions in small groups over three weeks. Each training session lasted only two hours and featured a fun, "beanbag-throwing" game involving two competitive teams. Armed with these simple techniques, the people were then ready and able to undertake small process improvement projects by themselves.

A salutary learning for us during our involvement was to realize how fast that business needed to move to stay ahead in the gaming market, and how short their product development cycles needed to be. We had initially facilitated formulation of "Action Plans" to deliver each strategic Objective over three years. We discovered that agility was more important.

The company subsequently placed emphasis on implementing quarterly Projects aligned to their original 3-Year Objectives. Rather than trying to deliver each Objective over three years by a 3-year set of scheduled "Actions", each quarter they identified and implemented the next priority quarterly Project to gain traction.

This was a tipping point in the development of our MBE approach for business transformation. We realized that we too had to anticipate and react to emerging changes in the marketplace by changing our own processes. Ever since, we have asked each new client to choose the planning horizon they feel is best suited to their needs—one, two, three, or even five years—and focused on execution of their strategic Objectives through incremental, iterative quarterly projects.

Strategic Planning Methodology

Here's how it's done...

We begin by updating the three major steps presented earlier (refer Figure 11) for strategy formulation and execution. In Figure 20, the two types of quarterly "Projects" are given their full titles as "*Standard* Projects" and "*FPI* Projects", where FPI stands for Fast Process Improvement.

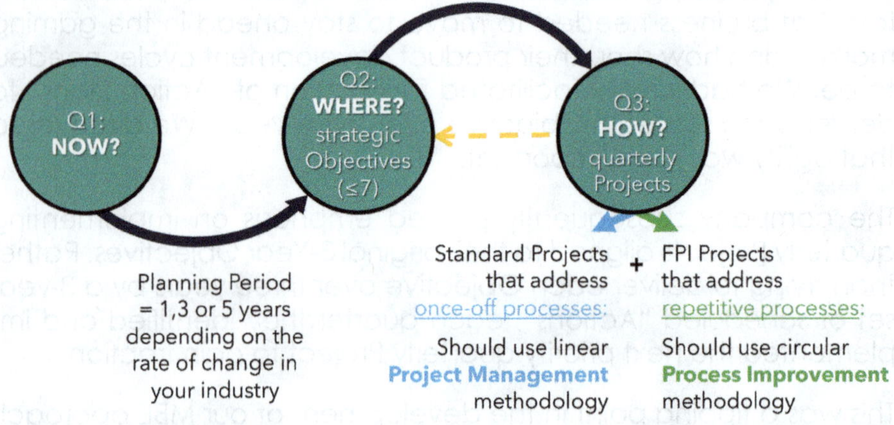
Q1:
NOW?
Q2:
WHERE?
strategic
Objectives
(≤7)
Q3:
HOW?
quarterly
Projects
Planning Period
= 1,3 or 5 years
depending on the
rate of change in
your industry
Standard Projects
that address
once-off processes:
Should use linear
Project Management
methodology
+
FPI Projects
that address
repetitive processes:
Should use circular
Process Improvement
methodology

Figure 20: Three key questions and answers lead to your 1-page Strategic Plan plus quarterly Standard Projects and FPI Projects to deploy each strategic Objective

Let's now dig deeper into the strategic planning process.

The world's most popular approach to developing a sound strategy features the four "perspectives" (layers) of Kaplan and Norton's *Balanced Scorecard* published in 1992 for *measurement* of strategy[24] and the subsequent *Strategy Map* developed by Mobil in 2001 for *formulation* of strategy consistent with the same four Kaplan and Norton perspectives[25].

This combination of four perspectives yields a Strategic Plan that is depicted graphically on one page. This simplicity combined with its completeness is why the CEOs of SMEs like it. It also leads to a powerful way of managing the risks that accompany each resultant strategic Objective.

Figure 21 shows an example of a 1-page Strategic Plan linked directly to the 1-page Process Model that was presented earlier for the steel fabrication business.

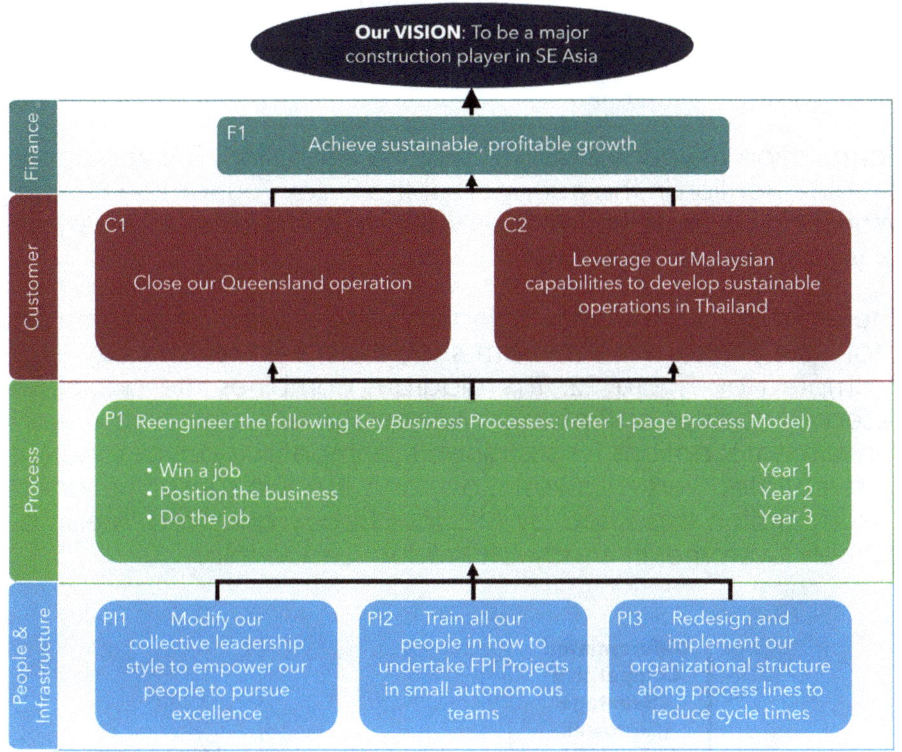

Figure 21: Example of a 1-page, 3-year Strategic Plan via the four Balanced Scorecard perspectives of Kaplan and Norton

Your 1-page Strategic Plan is developed from the top down. We recommend that your full Management Team develops the Strategic Plan at a 2-day Foundation Planning Workshop that marks the start of your journey towards full business excellence.

At the beginning of each year thereafter, a 1-day workshop is enough to review and roll your Strategic Plan forward by 12 months. In between these annual updates, the 1-page Strategic Plan is quickly reviewed for its on-going validity by the Management Team at their quarterly Planning Meetings.

Formulating your VISION

At the top of the 1-page Strategic Plan is your long-term VISION. It should describe as precisely as possible what you and your Management Team collectively agree is the company's customer-focused "Winning Aspiration" as defined in the book *PLAYING TO WIN by Lafley and Martin*[26]. The time-frame for your VISION should be at least twice as long as your strategic planning time-frame.

Formulation of your VISION (or Winning Aspiration) is given considerable attention in the early part of the 2-day Foundation Planning Workshop because your VISION will drive the choices for every one of your strategic Objectives.

Therefore, as a pre-cursor to finalizing your Vision, we recommend that your Management Team should address several key issues prompted by Figure 22. This diagram combines the acclaimed research findings of Professor Michael Porter[27] regarding the two fundamental options for sustainable competitive advantage (i.e., Differentiated versus Lowest Cost) and the two subset options for Differentiation espoused by Michael Treacy and Fred Wiersma[28], namely Customer Intimacy OR Product Leadership.

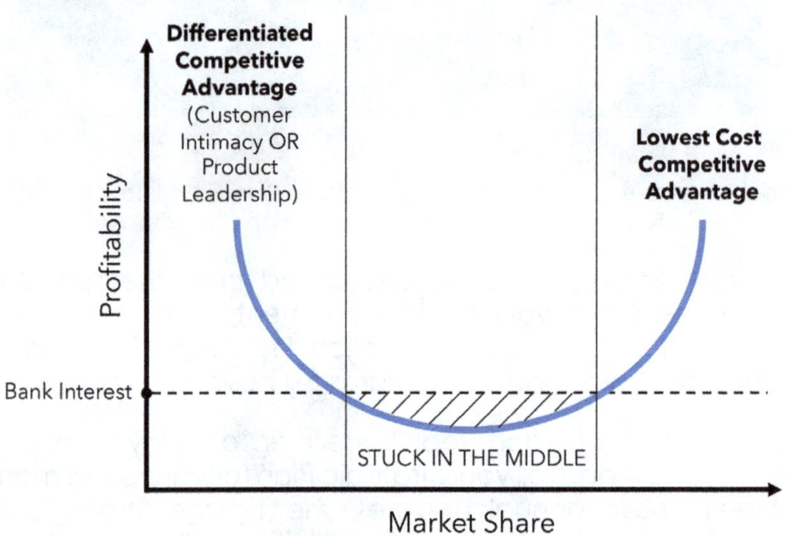

Figure 22: The danger of being STUCK IN THE MIDDLE if you don't have a clear Competitive Advantage

According to Porter, **Cost Leadership** and **Differentiation** are such fundamentally contradictory strategies, that any business attempting to combine them would end up being "stuck in the middle" and hence fail to enjoy superior profitability.

Cost Leadership requires standardized products or services with few unique or distinctive features, so that costs are kept to an absolute minimum.

On the other hand, **Differentiation** usually depends on offering customers unique benefits and features, which almost always increase production and marketing costs. The products or services on offer are priced accordingly so that good margins are realized.

> *"A business 'stuck in the middle' either loses the high-volume customers who demand low prices or must bid away its profits to get this business away from low-cost firms. Yet it also loses high-margin businesses—the cream—to the firms who are focused on high-margin targets or have achieved differentiation overall. The firm stuck in the middle also probably suffers from a blurred corporate culture and a conflicting set of organizational arrangements and motivation system."*
>
> Michael E Porter

There is no sustainable competitive advantage for a company that is stuck in the middle.

We believe that very few SMEs can win with the **Cost Leadership** strategy. One of the main reasons for this is that they generally lack the necessary economies of scale, and hence leave themselves open to attack by a larger competitor that can undercut the company's prices for the same type of goods or services. This leaves only the **Differentiation** option for most SMEs.

And according to Treacy and Wiersma[28], there are only two options within Porter's **Differentiation** option for sustainable competitive advantage. Their main premise is that a business must choose—and then achieve—market leadership in either **Customer Intimacy** or **Product Leadership**. They argue that a business must achieve market leadership for one of these competitive advantages and perform adequately for the other one at reasonable cost.

The **Customer Intimacy** strategy focuses on offering a unique range of customer goods or services that allows for the personalization of service and the customization of products to meet differing customer needs. Often, businesses that pursue this strategy bundle their products and services into a "solution" tailored to suit a specific customer. These businesses must be quick to learn about emerging customer needs and quick to find ways of satisfying them. In other words, they must become Agile.

Amazon and Salesforce are examples of Customer Intimacy.

The **Product Leadership** strategy aims to build a culture that continually brings superior products to market. These businesses achieve premium market prices due to the superior experience they create for their customers. Product Leaders recognize that excellence in creativity, problem-solving, and teamwork is critical to their success.

The disciplines they develop include:

- Research into emerging customer needs
- Teamwork
- Product management
- Marketing
- Talent management
- Knowledge management

Apple, Nike and Rolex are examples of Product Leadership.

So, how does all this help you formulate your VISION? During the 2-day Foundation Planning Workshop conducted within the first few weeks of your implementation, your Management Team (including you) should address these fundamental questions:

1. Where does your business currently sit on the curve of Figure 22?
2. Does your business have any chance of becoming and remaining the Lowest Cost producer of its offerings in the future?
3. If you believe your competitive advantage will be in Differentiation, will it be in terms of Customer Intimacy OR Product Leadership?
    - If Customer Intimacy, what would this require of the business in relation to your future customers over the long term?
    - If Product Leadership, what would this require of your future offerings over the long term?

If you choose Customer Intimacy, check out these key points for your consideration prior to attending the Workshop[29]...

"Customer intimacy is a highly customer-centric strategy, in which an organization strives to build a lasting personal relationship with its customers, by continually customizing its offerings to meet their exact needs and wants.

It can be a risky, high-cost strategy, as it requires a whole organization to buy into putting the customer's experience before the bottom line. It also focuses a lot of time, attention and resources on individual customers, or on small segments of a market.

You can take four steps to develop customer intimacy: empower your team members, use data effectively, narrow your customer focus, and explore outside partnerships.

It's essential to have a corporate structure that allows you to collect, analyze and act on data. The ability to understand or anticipate your customers' needs will encourage them to forge a long-term relationship with you, because of your dedication and unique ability in meeting those needs."

Based on the responses, your Management Team can now formulate your brief, long-term VISION. In stark contrast to your *clinical* ROLE statement at the top of your 1-page Process Model, your resultant VISION should be as *emotional* as possible. It should encapsulate your Winning Aspiration[26]—and be the reason why you and your people are keen to come to work every day. Being an emotional concept, it is of course, part of Leadership.

Incidentally, there is no set format for your VISION, but it must be brief so that your people find it easy to remember. And it should be unique to your business and NOT repeat elements of your ROLE statement which you already will have at the top of your 1-page Process Model.

It might help if you start your VISION with "To...," and the words that follow should be such that everybody in your organization can sense at any time in the future that the business has made real progress towards its achievement.

Here are a few generic examples as thought starters:

- "To be uppermost in the minds of Millennials when buying a product in our market"

- "To leverage our scale and become the lowest cost producer"
- "To have more current patents than anybody else in our targeted markets"
- "To have the highest customer satisfaction ratings for customized offerings in our chosen segments"
- "To engage and retain the most creative people involved in industrial design"

Formulating your Strategic Objectives

The Finance Objective is identified first, consistent with the organization's VISION = Winning Aspiration for the long term. In the example of Figure 21, the wording of the Finance Objective is adopted often by our clients. The quantification of "How *much* growth?"[26] would be specified in the KPIs that accompany this Objective.

Since the total number of Objectives should be no greater than seven to ensure the entire Strategic Plan is easy to remember, the Finance layer of the 1-page Strategic Plan should contain only one Objective.

The Customer Objectives are formulated next because the external customers are the source of the organization's revenues which directly impact financial success for the business. In combination, your 1-3 Customer Objectives should focus on "Where to Play"[26] which includes what to offer. They will reflect your choices for market segmentation, distribution channels, product categories, or geographical focus.

The *single* Process Objective is next since the Key Business (value-adding) Processes deliver the organization's goods or services to its external customers. This Objective should focus on "How to Win"[26]. Here, you simply list your highest priority Key Business Processes that must be re-engineered (from scratch) during the planning period to best support the previously determined Customer and Finance Objectives. A final adjustment of the BPR priorities imported from your 1-page Process Model may be necessary to ensure alignment with the preceding Customer and Finance Objectives and to ensure that, taken together, they address "How to Win."

Finally, the People & Infrastructure Objectives are formulated to enable the organization's processes to perform brilliantly. People & Infrastructure Objectives form the foundation of your Strategic Plan. They may need to address either your "Critical Capabilities"[26] (e.g., training for FPI Projects; training for Process Managers; switching to a process-oriented organizational structure,) or they may need to address "Required Systems"[26] (e.g., new IT system; robotics installation; factory layout; office infrastructure; reward and recognition system).

Summary Features of the MBE Strategic Planning Methodology

Let's recap on the features of this simple and direct way of doing strategic planning:

1. The long-term VISION statement should be brief and as emotional as possible. VISION is a leadership concept and should state the Winning Aspiration for the business—to be achieved through the collective efforts of all its employees. Perhaps you've heard the statement that if you want people to build an ark, don't talk to them about cutting trees and hammering nails, but instead instill in them a deep longing for the sea.

2. To keep the Strategic Plan easy for all employees to memorize for their day-to-day decision-making, and to keep the plan current during monthly reviews, it should consist of no more than seven Objectives. Most of our MBE clients have just five or six.

3. The "Finance" category is at the top because financial performance is the ultimate survival test for the organization and a tangible manifestation of its Winning Aspiration over the planning period. If finance is not healthy, the organization cannot invest adequately in any of the other three layers of the Balanced Scorecard.

4. The arrows connecting the Objectives describe the logical cause and effect flow of the diagram—from the bottom (causes) to the top (effects). The lower three layers of the diagram are necessary for the organization to achieve the Finance Objective and everything contributes to achievement of the overall VISION.

5. Every Objective of your Strategic Plan should be about fundamental change—not about the status quo. For example, no Objective should begin with the words: "Continue to..."

6. Every layer should contain at least one Objective so that the overall Strategic Plan has no major omissions. For example, a Strategic Plan with five Finance Objectives but no Objectives in any of the other three Balanced Scorecard layers cannot be implemented readily. Improved financial performance cannot be achieved through financial engineering alone.

7. The bullet points listed for the single Process Objective reflect:

   - The top priority process reengineering candidates from the organization's completed 1-page Process Model, PLUS
   - Any necessary adjustment to ensure alignment with the Customer and Finance Objectives

   Reminder: To avoid burdening the organization with too much change, a maximum of 1-2 BPR Projects should be planned and executed per annum during the planning period. Ideally, every Key Business (green) Process should be reengineered *at least every seven years* to prevent it from becoming outdated in today's rapidly changing business environment.

Further Examples of 1-page Strategic Plans

Several examples of 1-page Strategic Plans for different business types are presented in Appendix C.

Monitoring Delivery of your Strategic Objectives via KPIs

Figure 23 portrays our tabular format for documenting the full set of KPIs for your Strategic Plan. As indicated in the last column, this example is for a 3-Year Strategic Plan. The KPIs for F1 and P1 are indicative only.

Strategic Objective	Measure (#; $; %; Milestone)	Frequency (M;Q;B-A;Y)	Baseline Past End FY	3-year Target End FY
F1	***Achieve sustainable, profitable growth*** $ total national revenue (rolling past 12 months) % annual Return (EBIT) on Shareholder Funds	M Y	$12M 8%	$40M 15%
C1	***??*** ??	?	?	?
C2	***??*** ??	?	?	?
P1	***Reengineer the following Key Business Processes*** *(refer Process Model)* # BPR Projects completed per annum # FPI Projects completed per annum by each Process Manager	Y Y	0 0	2 4
PI1	***??*** ??	?	?	?
PI2	***??*** ??	?	?	?
PI3	***??*** ??	?	?	?

Add or delete rows to match the chosen ≤ 7 Objectives of your 1-page Strategic Plan

Figure 23: All your KPIs for strategic Objectives would be in this Table

A shorthand notation is used to denote each Objective. For instance, F1 refers to Financial Objective #1 and C1 and C2 refer to Customer Objective #1 and Customer Objective #2.

Since the Strategic Plan focuses on the end of the chosen planning period, target values in the last column need to be specified for the end of year one, two, three or five. Each Objective and its target values may of course be changed whenever the Strategic Plan is updated monthly or rolled forward by 12 months every year.

Relative to the operational KPIs of Figure 19, Figure 23 offers an extra milestone option for specifying the KPIs for strategic Objectives. For instance, in our example of the 3-Year Strategic Plan, the specified milestone for Objective PI3 could be: "Milestone: Have the new process-oriented organizational structure in place by end June 2022."

Following formulation and agreement on the strategic Objectives during the 2-day Foundation Planning Workshop, the Management Team may draft the most appropriate KPI(s) and target(s) that will be used to track the delivery of each Objective over the planning period. These draft KPIs are finalized after the Workshop.

Managing the Strategic Risks

After all the Objectives have been formulated, and during the 2-day Foundation Planning Workshop held within the first few weeks of your implementation, you will need to ensure that the risks associated with pursuing each Objective are believed to be manageable.

For SMEs, we have found the best way to handle risk management is to have it incorporated as an integral part of strategic planning and deployment rather than have it treated as a separate topic with its own set of bureaucratic controls such as a formal risk management committee with its own set of contingency plans.

Here is our recommended way forward:

For each Objective, ask the Management Team to determine the top three potential risks by following this simple procedure:

1. Brainstorm the big assumptions made when earlier formulating the Objective
2. Use a proven multi-voting technique to shortlist quickly the top three assumptions
3. Reword each of those three assumptions as a statement of risk that answers these 3 questions:
    - What could happen?
    - Why could it happen?
    - Why do we care?
4. Decide where each of these three risks fit on the Risk Assessment Matrix of Figure 24.

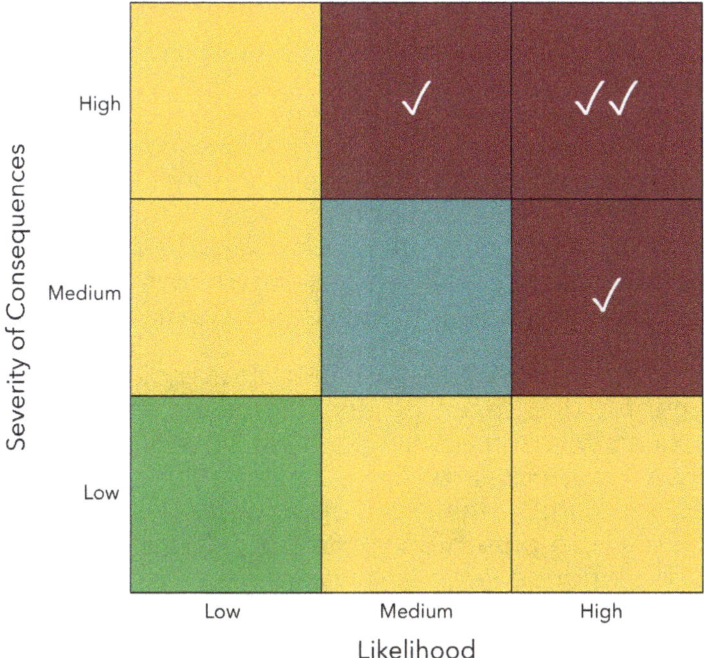

Figure 24: Risk Assessment Matrix

The intent is that specific mitigation steps will be taken via quarterly Projects for *only those risks that lie within the red squares of Figure 24.*

The Management Team then decides which Process Manager should be responsible for considering each red risk when formulating their top priority Standard Project or FPI Project every quarter. The obvious choice is YOU, because as the CEO you will be the Process Manager for the Key Support Process: "Govern and plan the business", and governance is concerned primarily with managing risk. It may be that other strategic or operational priorities prevail when you choose your quarterly Project, but you should never lose sight of the importance of managing the assigned risks over the planning period via the quarterly Project mechanism.

From Static to Dynamic Planning—the Key to Being Agile

Dynamic planning assumes that market conditions and internal circumstances change and so the Strategic Plan needs to change. It demands shorter planning cycles.

Our MBE approach to strategy execution incorporates dynamic planning. Every year the planning cycle restarts by having the Management Team formulate a rolling view of what the business would like to achieve over the chosen planning period. The time horizon for the rolling view is the chosen planning period.

In accordance with Figure 23, KPIs that indicate progressive achievement of the seven or less Objectives are tracked every quarter during the immediate year via your Strategic KPIs and monthly via the progress of the quarterly Projects. The data are input each month by the most appropriate Process Managers, and the results are presented graphically. This is done by your IT-Enabled Performance Reporting system.

Although the Objectives and their KPI targets are for the end of the entire planning period, the implementation focus is always on the next quarter via quarterly Projects.

Part of the Management Team's role at the Progress Review Meeting every month is to ensure that every Objective of the 1-page Strategic Plan remains current. Aided by the online Performance Reporting System, there is a continuous feedback loop for all involved.

Strategy Deployment Plus Operational Improvement via Local Autonomous Teams Implementing Quarterly Projects

All work, including strategy deployment, is done through the organization's Key Processes.

Deployment of strategic Objectives down and across the organization is done through the organization's agreed set of Key Processes depicted in the 1-page Process Model. Improving operations is also done by targeting the appropriate Key Processes.

Every quarter, each Process Manager chooses and sponsors ONE top-down quarterly project that will best contribute towards an

Objective that impacts their own assigned Key Process. In making their choice, the Process Manager should also consider any project that might be needed to assuage an associated strategic risk identified during the initial 2-day Foundation Planning Workshop.

In addition, every quarter, employees are encouraged by the Process Manager to put forward suggestions for ONE or more bottom-up quarterly projects aimed at operational improvements for their assigned Key Process. Provided these proposed bottom up Project(s) can be resourced by the available workforce, the Process Manager would sponsor the Project(s) each quarter in addition to the one top-down Project.

The Process Manager also identifies the *one* KPI that will best measure achievement of each adopted Project by the end of the quarter.

Figure 25 highlights these two types of quarterly Projects.

Figure 25: Deploying strategy and improving operations via top-down and bottom-up Quarterly Projects implemented by small autonomous teams

Finally, the Process Manager also decides whether each of their sponsored quarterly Projects is to be an FPI Project (for a local *repetitive* process) or a Standard Project (for a local *once-only* process). Most will be FPI Projects because repetitive processes in business are far more prevalent than once-only processes.

Every quarter, each Process Manager will go through this decision-making process and then follow through during the quarter to monitor progress for each Project (via its agreed KPI) and to support the teams "from above", upon request.

To avoid overload for individuals, the Management Team should ensure that no employee may be a member of more than one Project team per quarter.

All teams have a nominated Project Manager. The team members, including the Project Manager, all commit to being involved part-time during the quarter to complete their Project.

Figure 26 shows a worked example of the decision-making process undertaken by each Process Manager each quarter...

Key Process: Win a job Process Manager: Fred Ames
Relevant Objective: Obtain the majority of our Sales from our e-commerce website
KPI: % on-line Sales per month relative to total Sales | 1-year Target: 60%
Top Down Quarterly Project: Design and launch a new e-commerce site
[Standard Project] for a once-only process!
KPI: % complete, measured monthly | Quarterly Target: 100%
AND
Bottom Up Quarterly Project: Improve our 'Provide a Quotation' process
[FPI Project] for a repetitive process!
KPI: % Cycle Time reduction measured at end of quarter | Quarterly Target: 50%

Figure 26: Example of how a Process Manager translates a relevant Objective into a top-down quarterly Project and a bottom-up quarterly Project

Next, the Process Manager completes a standard 1-page Project Brief for their chosen quarterly Project(s). The Project Brief includes employee nominations for a small cross-functional team (3-8 people including the nominated Project Manager)—plus a facilitator in the case of an FPI Project. Team members should be chosen to ensure adequate representation of knowledge and experience for the targeted process.

Once an employee has taken part in at least one FPI Project, they usually have enough confidence to facilitate the standard 2-hour planning session for another FPI Project. There is no need to hire external facilitators for this purpose. See Appendix A: Further Resources for further information on the approach.

The Process Manager should encourage their teams to act autonomously over the quarter to deliver their Project. Performance of the Project each month as measured by their agreed KPI is reported by the team's Project Manager using the company's online Performance Reporting System.

Occasionally, depending on the nature and scope of a Standard Project, the duration may need to be longer than one quarter. This can be assessed on a case by case basis.

Further Deployment of Strategic Objectives Down to Individual Employees

Within each organizational unit, individual employee commitments are best established by asking each employee what they can do over each employee review period to influence and improve the delivery of one or more strategic Objectives and / or influence the performance of one or more Key Processes of the business.

By obtaining their agreement and monitoring their achievements against those commitments, you'll have achieved a full "line of sight" alignment of all performance indicators from the bottom of the organizational structure to the very top, as shown in Figure 27. Then you will indeed "get what you measure" and be well on your way to business success.

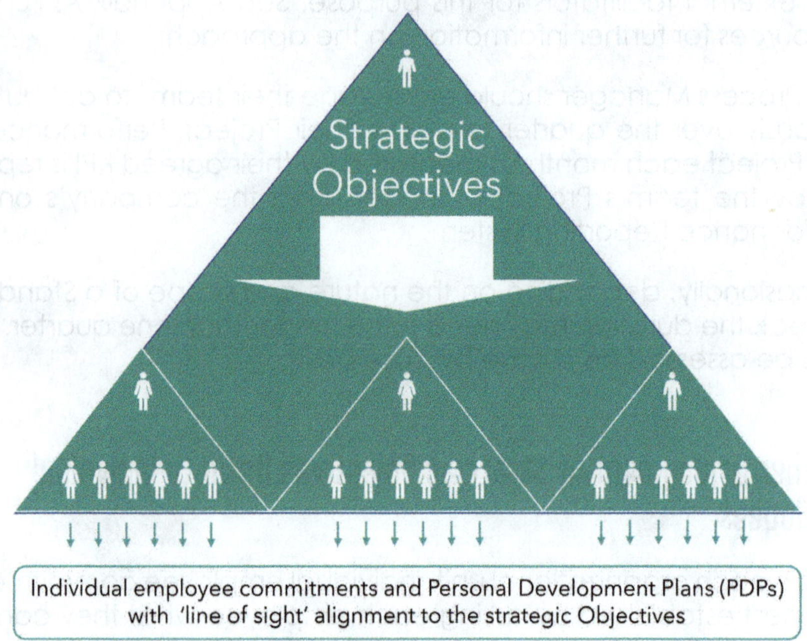

Figure 27: "Line of Sight" alignment of Objectives and individual commitments from bottom to top

PART 3:

IMPLEMENTING

MY BUSINESS EXCELLENCE®

Overview of the Four Implementation Phases

This book is all about practical implementation, and Figure 28 shows the four Implementation Phases for the entire MBE approach. The intent is for your business to have embedded the MBE approach as 'business as usual' and be well on the way to having a culture of continuous improvement by the end of Year 2.

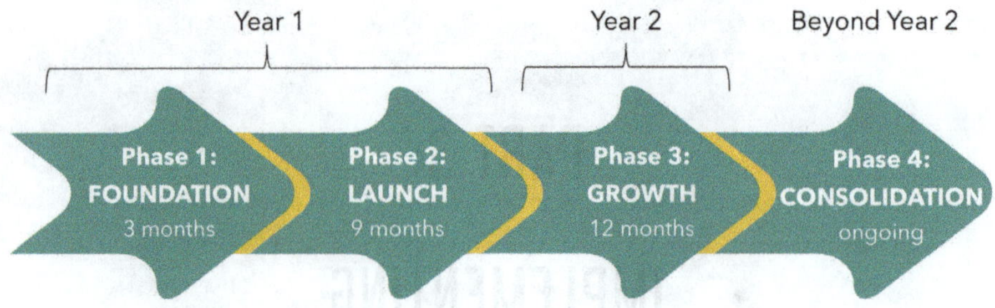

Figure 28: Four Implementation Phases—the fastest and most cost-effective road map to business excellence and organizational agility

This phased implementation ensures the benefits generated will far exceed all costs well within Year 1—with accelerating compound growth of net benefits thereafter.

The intensive **FOUNDATION** Phase over the first three months is the most critical because it sets up all five Prerequisites for excellence for implementation *and full integration* in the later Phases.

The **LAUNCH** Phase over three quarters begins by extending the training for FPI Projects beyond the Management Team to more employees. The trained employees then take part in a series of carefully targeted top-down quarterly Projects that progressively deploy each strategic Objective.

The **GROWTH** Phase is where quarterly bottom-up Projects for operational improvements are added to the ongoing top-down quarterly Projects and BPR Project(s) required for strategy deployment. The total number of quarterly Projects undertaken in this phase is far greater than for the previous LAUNCH Phase.

After your business completes the steps required for the GROWTH Phase, you will be ready to enter the **CONSOLIDATION** Phase. At that point, the business should be fully familiar with all the MBE techniques and they will have been embedded into business operations as "Business As Usual".

As your business progresses through these four phases, the measurable nt benefits will compound dramatically.

Let's now explore each implementation phase in some detail...

FOUNDATION Phase 1 (3 months)

This phase is most intensive for the full Management Team. The CEO must be fully committed and prepared to lead the charge. Furthermore, the CEO and other people in managerial roles need to have, or be developing, a collective leadership style that empowers employees to work in small, autonomous teams to get things done.

With reference to Figure 6, if you have a collective *autocratic* (does TO people) or *hero* (does FOR people) leadership style, and you are not prepared to change, then the MBE approach is clearly not for you or your business. The ideal leadership style is either *coach* (does WITH people) or *enabler* (does THROUGH people). Success with the MBE approach is dependent on getting all your people excited about and engaged in improving the business. Developing a culture of continuous improvement throughout your businesses must come from the top.

SME businesses that don't have a formal but dynamic strategy have no chance of becoming excellent performers. In a similar vein, SME businesses that DO formulate a strategy but don't follow through by ensuring key stakeholders take ownership with well-orchestrated implementation mechanisms are likely to have the strategy gather dust in a drawer.

The first month focuses on formulation of your 1-page Process Model and your 1-page Strategic Plan with its associated risks. The right KPIs required to measure the operational plus strategic health of the business every month are set, together with arrangements for Performance Reporting, Project Management and Knowledge Management. Towards the end of this first month, basic training for the entire Management Team in the "how to" techniques of FPI Projects is undertaken.

During months 2-3, a few carefully chosen FPI Projects are undertaken involving members of the Management Team and aimed at ensuring the business is all set to enter the LAUNCH Phase with all the key players on board.

Progress for each of these first projects is monitored by the Management Team at the inaugural monthly Progress Review Meeting, together with monitoring of progress against each project's KPI.

2-day Foundation Planning Workshop

This intense workshop involves all members of your Management Team and occurs at the beginning of the FOUNDATION Phase.

If you sense that there may be one or two outstanding employees that have the potential to join the Management Team in the next year or so, you should also invite them to participate in this crucial workshop. Along with the other participants, they would automatically become candidates for appropriate Process Manager roles.

Developed during this Workshop, your Strategic Plan will be depicted graphically on a single page. The strategy contains a clear, long-term VISION, followed by seven or less strategic Objectives. Depending on the perceived rate of change in your industry, the horizon for your strategic plan may be one, two, three, or five years out.

Strategy formulation with associated risk management control forms the major component of this Workshop. Along the way, the Management Team develops its agreed 1-page Process Model of the entire business operation, because all work in the business—including deployment of the strategy—is done through its key processes. The agreed 1-page Process Model depicts a clear statement of the company's ROLE plus all the Key Business Processes (for external Customers) and all the Key Support Processes (for internal Customers = your own employees).

A willing part-time Process Manager from the Management Team (possibly augmented by one or two other invitees) is assigned to each Key Process during the Workshop.

Towards the end of the Workshop, we recommend that the Management Team is trained fully in how to plan and implement

FPI Projects. This helps each Process Manager understand the benefits and what's involved when doing this later in a practical setting. We have found the best way to do this training within two hours is by having two small teams compete against each other at throwing bean bags towards a target. This is a fun simulation of a process in action. The techniques used to improve accuracy of the bean bag throws are the same as those required to improve any real work process. For further details about our Beanbag FPI training kit, see Appendix A: Further Resources.

Finally, the Management Team chooses a few simple FPI Projects needed to begin strategy deployment immediately following this Workshop. Every member of the Management Team participates in one of these projects which must be completed before the end of the FOUNDATION Phase. These projects enable Management Team members to master the FPI techniques and to be seen by the rest of the organization as leading by example for what is to come in the following phases.

Agenda for the 2-day Foundation Planning Workshop

You will have gathered by now that the 3-month FOUNDATION Phase is critical to getting things off to a good start. At the front is the 2-day Foundation Planning Workshop involving the entire Management Team full-time.

In case you are wondering about what you will be doing during these 2 days, Figure 29 shows the Agenda for this crucial Workshop:

Day 1 (from 8.30 am start until 6.00 pm close - with 20 min Morning Tea at 10.30am, Lunch at 12.45 pm for 45 min and 20 min Afternoon Tea at 2.30pm)
• Introductions and welcome • A brief overview of what it takes to be excellent in business - the proven, simplified (memorable!) 5-Prerequisite business excellence framework which will be used to develop our strategy and to plan its implementation • Agreement on the strategic Planning Period (i.e., 1,3 or 5 years) • A brief explanation of how best to get Shared Strategic Direction via the simple Balanced Scorecard planning sequence of four perspectives: Finance; Customer; Process; People & Infrastructure • Identification of our Ideal Customer Segment Agreement with direct implications for our ROLE and VISION (Winning Aspiration) • Strategic ranking of our top Strengths, Weaknesses, Opportunities and Threats • Strategic ranking of the top Expectations of each Key Stakeholder Group • Development of the agreed ROLE statement (clinical) for our business (Level 0 Process!) – i.e., What we do for a living • Development of the agreed VISION statement (emotional) for our business – i.e., What we believe "Winning" will mean for the business in the longer term (i.e., at least for twice the Planning Period) • Development of our complete Process Model (Level 1 processes) - for regular business operations - on 1 page • Identification of the ideal Process Manager for each of our Key Processes - plus an understanding of their crucial role in deploying strategy and continually improving the business • Identification of our 'most broken' Key Processes to be completely re-engineered as an integral part of our Strategic Plan • Pictorial development of the draft Strategic Plan via the four Balanced Scorecard perspectives - on 1 page
Day 2 (from 8.30 am start until 6.00 pm close) - with the same 'breaks' as for Day 1
• Identification and quantification of the Risks associated with each strategic Objective. • Fast Process Improvement training for all attendees • Outline of the importance of doing occasional 'top-down' Process Reengineering projects and frequent 'bottom-up' Fast Process Improvement projects - with Cycle Time reduction as the main game for our business • Formulation of the key quarterly Projects to deploy our new strategy • Immediate Next Steps to a) Finalize the workshop deliverables and b) Begin implementation and monitoring of progress against the Strategic Plan

Figure 29: Agenda for the 2-day Foundation Planning Workshop

Following the Foundation Planning Workshop (approximately 10 weeks)

All the high-level strategic and operational KPIs are set after the workshop following one-to-one discussions with each Process Manager.

In all three following phases, the assigned Process Managers are accountable for deploying the strategic Objectives and for effecting local operational improvements via measurable quarterly Projects. For this reason, special emphasis during the FOUNDATION Phase is placed on training the nominated Process Managers in their new part-time role.

During this period, employees are trained in groups of 10-12 in the FPI techniques using the same bean bag process simulation described above for the Management Team.

Seven Pivotal Process Manager Roles

Figure 30 shows the tight linkages between the seven Key Support Processes and the MBE Reference Framework for excellence.

MBE Reference Framework

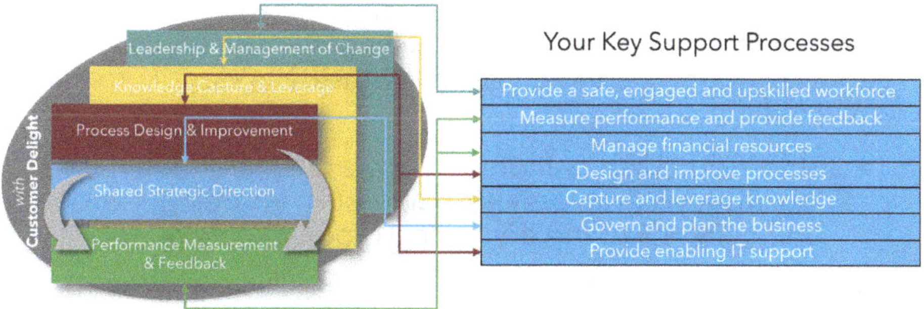

Figure 30: Your seven Key Support Processes link to the MBE Framework, and their Process Managers have a critical role to play

<u>Note</u>: Multiple Process Manager roles may be assigned to one member of the Management Team if the enterprise is very small (i.e., 10-50 employees).

The Process Managers of these seven Key Support Processes are not merely looking after shared services on demand as in most SMEs today. You and they must prioritize working ON the business over working IN the business and communicate that priority throughout the company. It is essential that individual employees in the shared services units (e.g., Finance; HR; IT) are made available by their line managers (also Process Managers) when called upon by other Process Managers to take part in part-time quarterly Projects.

In addition, these Process Managers need to choose their *own* quarterly FPI Projects and Standard Projects to help deploy the strategic Objectives and improve their assigned Key Support Processes. In this respect, these Process Managers are no different from the organization's other Process Managers—but with two notable exceptions...

Exception 1: The Process Manager for both "Design and improve processes" and "Capture and leverage knowledge" will report directly to the CEO and will not normally have any staff. Their role is unique:

- Become the facilitator of all the company's future BPR Projects following the LAUNCH Phase
- Train employees in the FPI methodology either via the beanbag simulation or by direct participation in FPI projects
- Coach the Project Managers of FPI Projects and Standard Projects in their responsibilities for project execution, including proper implementation of the QA Wedge for each Project
- Be the guardian of the company's overall QMS, overseeing the way it is progressively being built, including the quality and currency of the contained process knowledge
- If desired, assist the CEO in obtaining ISO 9001:2015 certification of the company's established QMS and overall management system
- Become the company's in-house source of knowledge regarding the ongoing MBE approach to implementation of business excellence and organizational agility

Not surprisingly, most SMEs do not have a suitably experienced person ready and able to take on this role from day one. In such cases, what normally happens is that the Management Team nominates an existing employee *outside* the Management Team that they believe has the potential to grow into this full-time role over time. The nominated person is often relatively young with a strong IT background and should be excited at the opportunity to show what they are capable of.

Exception 2: The Process Manager for "Measure performance and provide feedback" is responsible for ensuring that the high level KPIs are properly updated and reported every month. The CEO usually takes this Process Manager role in addition to the Process Manager role for "Govern and plan the business".

You accelerate adoption of the approach across the board by making involvement in the MBE process fun and rewarding. Planning Meetings and Progress Review Meetings can be just as productive if not more so when held in an informal, relaxed atmosphere rather than in a boardroom with slide presentations. For overworked employees enmired at the coalface, these sessions can be a welcome break from the everyday routine, and proof that the company values their insight and input. They become a great morale-boosting tool. Then, of course, there are the end-of-Project celebrations (refer PDCA Cycle later in this book) that reinforce the perceived value of the work done ON the business.

At review time (once or twice per year,) individual employee commitments should be established by asking the employee what they can do to help implement an Objective and / or help improve a Key Process. Similarly, their Personal Development Plan (PDP) for the next review period should be framed in this same context. For example, an employee may wish to undertake part-time study of techniques for reducing the Cycle Time in business processes. Another employee might seek support for completing a course leading to a formal qualification relevant to the business. Yet another employee may wish to become a recognized facilitator of multiple FPI Projects on behalf of the organization.

By obtaining employee agreement and then monitoring employee achievements against their commitments, you will be well on your way to business success.

Key Points for Phase 1

1. The 2-day Foundation Planning Workshop occurs at the beginning of the 3-month duration of this phase. The main deliverables of the Foundation Workshop are the 1-page Process Model for RUNNING your business and the 1-page Strategic Plan for CHANGING your business.

2. Your developed Strategic Plan becomes a clear roadmap for what the business will achieve over the planning period. You will review your strategy and its KPIs every month, and you will formally roll the strategy forward once every year. Your strategy will of course need to change over time, but that's no excuse for not having one to guide your journey.

3. You must ensure your key people take ownership of all the Key Processes of your business and understand their crucial roles as Process Managers—and you should lead by example.

4. You should have the right infrastructure in place for Performance Reporting, Project Management, and Knowledge Management. Without it, you're going to have to work much harder each month to measure your progress and document your process changes in later phases.

5. Following the Foundation Planning Workshop, you will need to get buy-in to your Strategic Plan from all employees, and from the board (if applicable). In other words, you need to make sure everyone is pulling the same way and making consistent day-to-day decisions.

6. Following the Workshop, you and your Management Team will finalize the high-level set of KPIs for all strategic Objectives and for all Key Processes and begin measuring progress against all of them every month at the Progress Review Meeting.

Activity Schedule for Phase 1

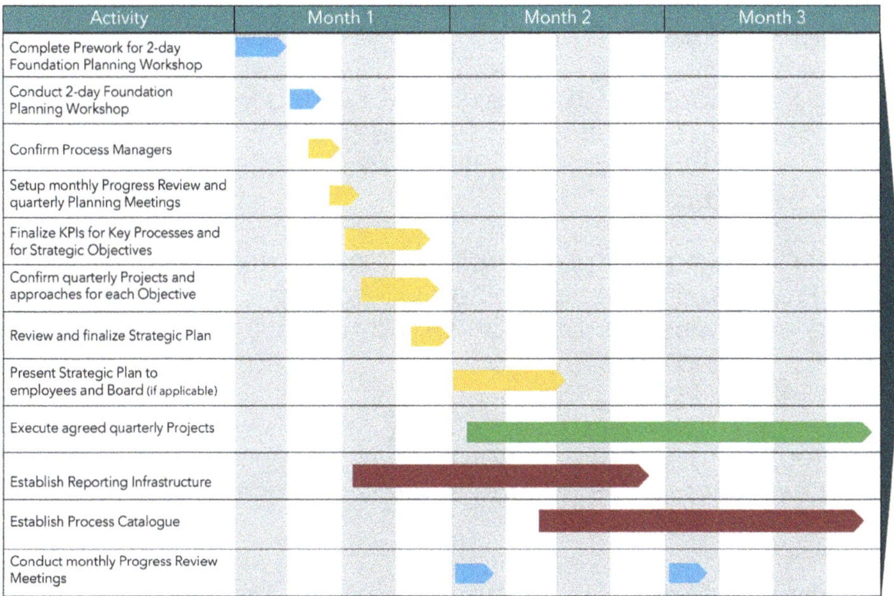

Activity
Month 1
Month 2
Month 3
Complete Prework for 2-day Foundation Planning Workshop
Conduct 2-day Foundation Planning Workshop
Confirm Process Managers
Setup monthly Progress Review and quarterly Planning Meetings
Finalize KPIs for Key Processes and for Strategic Objectives
Confirm quarterly Projects and approaches for each Objective
Review and finalize Strategic Plan
Present Strategic Plan to employees and Board (if applicable)
Execute agreed quarterly Projects
Establish Reporting Infrastructure
Establish Process Catalogue
Conduct monthly Progress Review Meetings

Figure 31: Activity Schedule for the FOUNDATION Phase (3 months)

LAUNCH Phase 2 (9 months)

During this LAUNCH Phase, the rubber hits the road. You begin to execute your strategy in full.

The Process Managers of your seven Key Support Processes will be the main drivers of progress, backed up by the Process Managers of the Key Business Processes.

In this phase you'll begin to build momentum by conducting monthly Progress Review Meetings and quarterly Planning Meetings and executing your strategy through quarterly Projects.

Each quarterly project team is autonomous and led by an assigned part-time Project Manager. Every month during this phase, the Management Team monitors the progress of each part-time project team and also monitors overall progress against the agreed KPIs for delivery of each Objective.

At the end of each quarter, new top-down strategy deployment Projects with part-time team members and assigned part-time Project Managers are configured and briefed by the Process Managers for the next quarter.

During this phase, the business may also undertake at least one BPR Project for a Key Business Process that requires fundamental reform. For a very small SME with less than 50 employees, this step should be bypassed.

You will realize positive net benefits within just a few months through these Projects. Efficiencies gained will free up time for the participating employees so they can spend more time working on the business, freeing up even more time. This creates a positive "flywheel" effect. Exciting Stuff.

Importantly, the benefits generated by the end of Year 1 will be well in excess of all internal and external implementation costs.

Key Points for Phase 2

1. Your Process Managers are the engine room for implementing business excellence. They need to be trained for success and held accountable by you, the CEO.

2. More employees are trained in FPI techniques by using the "bean bag" process simulation over 2 hours in groups of 10-12 employees.

3. Throughout this LAUNCH Phase, your Objectives begin to be deployed via an increasing number of targeted, top-down quarterly FPI Projects or Standard Projects sponsored by a few of the Process Managers. Each Process Managers chooses and defines their quarterly Project(s) to best contribute to delivery of one strategic Objective. There are two constraints to the number of Projects given the green light:

    - No employee should be involved in more than one Project.

    - There should be enough employees available to populate the chosen Projects.

4. The average Benefit : Cost ratio for these quarterly Projects should exceed 10 : 1 and the efficiencies gained will help free up your company's resources to make further improvements.

5. Provided your business has more than 50 full time employees, you'll trigger your first major Business Process Reengineering (BPR) Project during this phase.
6. Each month a Progress Review Meeting will occur to review the progress of each quarterly Project, Key Processes and their respective KPIs to ensure everything remains on track.
7. Each quarter a Planning Meeting will occur to review the strategic Objectives and select new quarterly Projects to further progress your strategic Objectives.
8. By means of a 1-day Strategic Planning Workshop held at the end of Year 1, your 1-page Strategic Plan will be formally reviewed and rolled forward to reflect any major changes required.

Activity Schedule for Phase 2

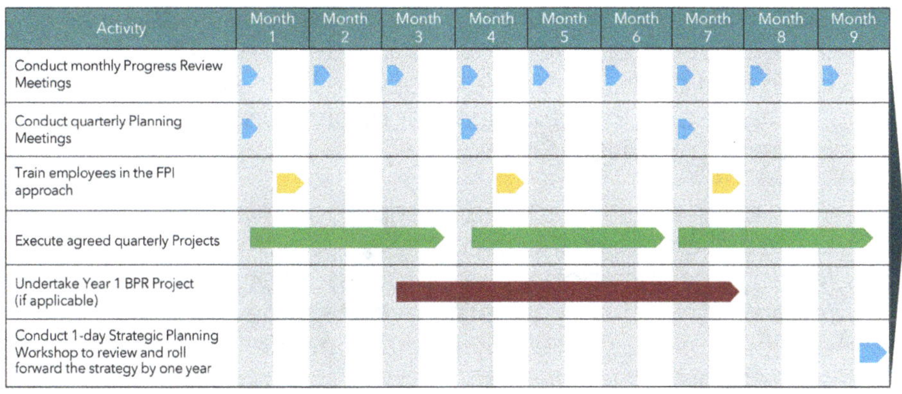

Activity
Month 1
Month 2
Month 3
Month 4
Month 5
Month 6
Month 7
Month 8
Month 9
Conduct monthly Progress Review Meetings
Conduct quarterly Planning Meetings
Train employees in the FPI approach
Execute agreed quarterly Projects
Undertake Year 1 BPR Project (if applicable)
Conduct 1-day Strategic Planning Workshop to review and roll forward the strategy by one year

Figure 32: Activity Schedule for the LAUNCH Phase (9 Months)

GROWTH Phase 3 (Year 2)

In this GROWTH Phase, you will disseminate and leverage the knowledge and skills needed to implement the approach throughout your business. Many more of your employees will become progressively engaged with the same techniques already introduced in the FOUNDATION and LAUNCH phases. Your leaders will continue to nurture and empower their employees using these proven techniques.

This Phase includes a mechanism to ensure that no employee is involved in more than one quarterly Project (either top-down or bottom-up) or BPR Project at any one time. Further employee training for FPI Projects will be necessary to enable the rapidly expanding number of quarterly Projects underway during this phase.

Many experts estimate it takes years to instill a new culture, particularly in very large businesses. However, our MBE techniques designed exclusively for SMEs enable a culture of continuous improvement to be instilled much faster. By the end of Year 2, you will be well on your way because most of your employees will have been actively involved each quarter in improving the processes of the business and progressively achieving the strategic Objectives.

Key Points for Phase 3

1. Dependent on the number of Key Processes in the business, the number of quarterly Projects undertaken in this phase will be limited by the available people resources but certainly will be far greater than the number of projects completed in the preceding LAUNCH Phase.
2. Your quarterly Projects will comprise a mixture of top-down strategy deployment projects selected by your Process Managers and bottom-up process improvement projects recommended by your employees at the coal face of operations and approved by their respective Process Manager.
3. You will also undertake one or two large, top-down BPR Projects.
4. By the end of this Phase, you will see a culture of continuous improvement beginning to flourish within your business as employees throughout your business take ownership of improvement initiatives.
5. At the end of Year 2, your 1-page Strategic Plan will again be formally reviewed and rolled forward during a 1-day Strategic Planning Workshop to reflect any major changes required.

Activity Schedule for Phase 3

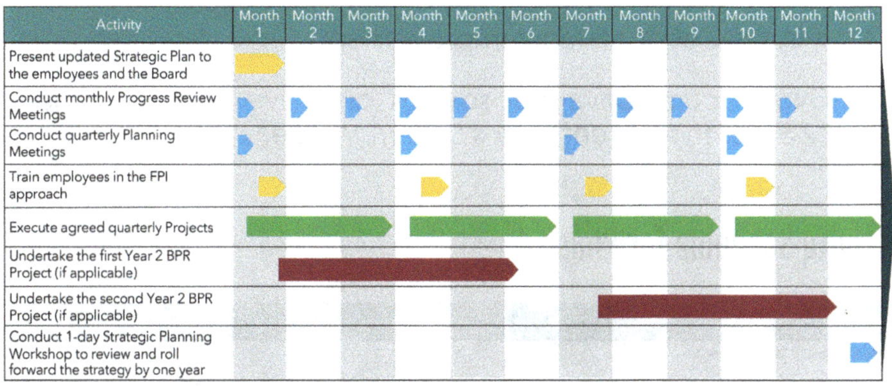

Activity
Month 1
Month 2
Month 3
Month 4
Month 5
Month 6
Month 7
Month 8
Month 9
Month 10
Month 11
Month 12
Present updated Strategic Plan to the employees and the Board
Conduct monthly Progress Review Meetings
Conduct quarterly Planning Meetings
Train employees in the FPI approach
Execute agreed quarterly Projects
Undertake the first Year 2 BPR Project (if applicable)
Undertake the second Year 2 BPR Project (if applicable)
Conduct 1-day Strategic Planning Workshop to review and roll forward the strategy by one year

Figure 33: Activity Schedule for GROWTH Phase (Year 2)

CONSOLIDATION Phase 4 (ongoing beyond Year 2)

This final, ongoing Phase is about building on what you have already achieved during the GROWTH Phase and institutionalizing the approach so that it becomes "business as usual". You will continue to deploy your strategy plus improve local processes via a mix of top-down and bottom-up quarterly Projects executed by small, autonomous teams. You should aim to have the whole workforce positively engaged in working ON the business approximately 5% of their available work time on average.

The CONSOLIDATION Phase is where you realize that your business has developed a continuous improvement culture. The business should be well on the way to being recognized externally for its high performance. As its CEO, you may come to be regarded as a leader in your industry.

Key Points for Phase 4

1. Successfully executing your strategy
2. Significant productivity gains through many FPI Projects, with an average Benefit to Cost Ratio of at least 10:1

3. Massive productivity gains and new capabilities added through BPR Projects
4. A culture of continuous improvement
5. Overall *cumulative* net savings after five years of at least 22.5% of *this current year's* Sales revenue.

Activity Schedule for Phase 4

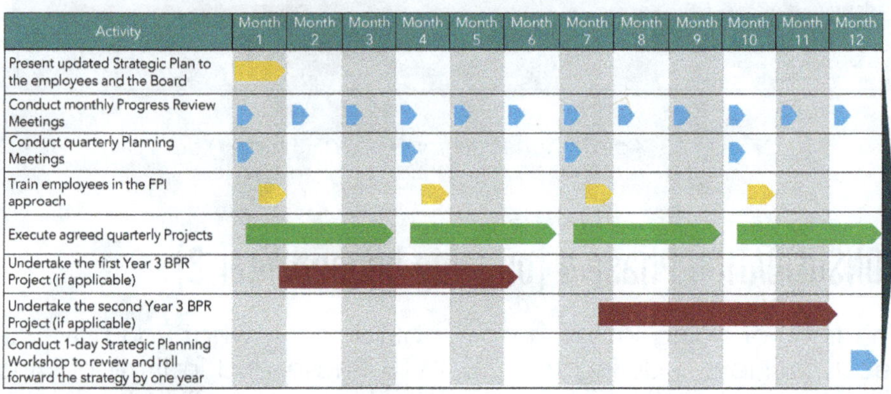

Figure 34: Activity Schedule for CONSOLIDATION Phase (Ongoing beyond Year 2)

Building a high-performing business is not easy and does not happen overnight, but with the systematic, step-by-step sequence outlined in Phases 1-4, you will get there.

In working your way through these four phases of implementation, you and your people will need to become familiar with multiple components and the common language used to refer to them.

Three Types of Projects

Implementing the MBE approach involves a combination of workshops and projects. The workshops are where you work ON your business, identifying the metrics to track, processes that need improvement, how those improvements are to be made, and who is responsible for sponsoring and tracking them. The projects are where you implement those planned changes within your business.

There are three types of projects:

1. **Quarterly (or longer) Standard Projects**—for once-only processes. These are managed using the traditional project management technique.

2. **Quarterly Fast Process Improvement (FPI) Projects**—for bottom-up business optimization and top-down strategy deployment via repetitive processes. Each is planned during a 2-hour workshop and is completed within eight weeks. These projects are designed to progressively deploy the company's strategic Objectives down and across the organization, or to fix niggling operational issues with existing workflows at the coalface or elsewhere. They are implemented by those employees whose job roles are most affected.

3. **Business Process Reengineering (BPR) Projects**—for top-down business optimization. They involve end-to-end reengineering of your repetitive Key Business Processes for your external customers. A BPR Project is triggered whenever the Management Team believes it's time for fundamental improvement in any one of its Key Business Processes. Because every Key Business Process is, by definition, highly significant for the well-being of business operations, fundamental reengineering will generate big positive implications for your business. This is why they must be included in your 1-page Strategic Plan. Each BPR Project is planned during a 2-day workshop. These projects usually take much longer than one quarter to implement. Depending on the complexity and scope of the target process, implementation may take between 3 and 18 months.

Standard Projects

Standard Projects are those which are important to the growth of the business, but which are not part of repetitive business operations; they result in one-off improvements. For example, a quarterly Standard Project may be triggered by a Process Manager who wishes to acquire and fit-out an office extension.

Children learn basic project management techniques from their parents. For example, a 10-year-old child may be told that playing a game on their iPad from 7 pm is not allowed unless their bed has been made, their discarded clothes have been placed in the drawer, and they have cleaned their teeth. Even at that early age, the child knows that to meet some time-based deadline, they must schedule and resource their activities. Most employees today have already been exposed to simple project management techniques many times over in their lives.

Scheduling of tasks in the right order is the essence of simple project management. Later in business life, employees may be exposed to more advanced versions of project management techniques, possibly aided by specialized software such as Microsoft Project or one of the many online offerings such as Basecamp or Asana. Please see Appendix A: Further Resources for further discussion on tooling and templates to assist with project management in general and process improvement projects in particular.

1-page Project Brief for a Standard Project

Ensuring scope creep is managed is one of the most important elements of defining and planning a project in our approach. Creating a Project Brief prior to the first planning session is the most effective way. Figure 35 shows our 1-page template for a Standard Project Brief. It is filled out by the sponsoring Process Manager and pulls together all the important information for the project on one page. It should be read by all participants nominated to attend the associated 2-hour Planning Workshop.

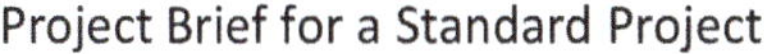
Project Brief for a Standard Project

Project Description

Relocate Head Office from Richmond to new premises in Clear Lake

Project Details

Project Background:
We currently are at full capacity for accommodating our Head Office staff. We have leased a suitable new office space in Clear Lake which should cater for our planned expansion over the next 5 years.

Dependencies:
We cannot move into the new premises until we have completed the fit-out to suit our needs. The lead time for telephone system installation and commissioning may be substantial and therefore needs to be scheduled early in the Action Plan.

Deliverables:
All staff relocated and ready for 'business as usual' by end June 2020, including car park provisioning

Stakeholders:
Our staff; Our suppliers; Our walk-in customers; Our fit-out contractor

Project Objective

Complete the relocation by the end of this quarter

KPI Specification ($#,$,%, Milestone):	*Target:*
Milestone: Relocation complete by quarter's end (30 June 2020)	Not applicable since a Milestone

Project Logistics

Project Sponsor (Process Manager):	*Team Members:*
Helen Roberts	Adrian Morgan, Paul Adler, Ashleigh Smith (Project Manager)

Meeting Arrangements i.e. for the 2-hour Planning Workshop plus subsequent team meetings:

Planning Workshop 3 April 2020, 9am – 11am in Meeting Room 4; At the discretion of the Project Manager, team meetings by remote or face to face every 1-2 weeks until the project is completed.

Figure 35: 1-page Project Brief template for a Standard Project

Fast Process Improvement (FPI) Projects

Each FPI Project improves a low-level process within the business that is recognized as having problems or is required to deploy a strategic Objective.

Top-down projects are triggered by a line manager or a Process Manager. Reminder: Not every line manager will also be a Process Manager.

Bottom-up projects may be triggered by any employee and are reviewed by the Process Manager for the related Key Process.

Each FPI Project is scheduled to take no longer than 8 weeks to complete. This includes the 2-hour Planning Workshop conducted at the beginning, and completion of the four Quality Assurance (QA) activities at the end (i.e., Document; Train; Measure; Celebrate).

Apart from the implementation of occasional employee suggestions for "Just-Do-It" operational improvements, FPI Projects are the main source of steady, incremental business improvement. They typically have a Benefit to Cost ratio of 10 : 1, although the ratio can often be as high as 100 : 1.

These huge returns for small process adjustments, combined with the ability to start and finish each FPI Project within a quarter, makes this one of the foundational techniques of the MBE approach. Quarterly FPI Projects are fun projects that generate a genuine team-based culture for all employees—provided they are done often enough.

Please remember: If a process is performing poorly, don't blame the people currently executing the process. This causes the criticized employees to shun their involvement in the proposed process improvement project. Instead, blame the process itself for being sub-optimal. That way you keep your involved employees positively engaged in making improvements and contributing to the culture of continuous improvement and knowledge sharing.

Here are three results of quarterly FPI Projects completed by three past clients:

FPI Example 1: Manufacture the product

The manufacturing industry has long recognized the benefits of process improvement.

Target Process	**Manufacture the product**
Problems	It took too long to produce each product i.e., long Cycle Time. There was a large backlog of partially completed products at different stages of the process due to bottlenecks.
Solution	Change the layout of the associated factory cell to minimize time lost to hand-offs between successive machining operations.
Benefit	The overall batch size moving through the process was reduced from 240 to 40 units, and Cycle Time was reduced by 35%. This yielded over $1M savings in working capital due to the permanent reduction in factory inventory levels.

FPI Example 2: Invoice the customer and collect the money

Cashflow issues are common for many businesses due to the excessive time it takes to get paid for their products or services.

Target Process	**Invoice the customer and collect the money**
Problem	Many invoices were greater than 60 days outstanding
Solution	Offer a direct debit option for recurring invoices
Benefit	There was a 25% reduction of days outstanding down to an average of 45 days.

FPI Example 3: Answer the phone

Cost reduction isn't the only trigger for improving a process via an FPI Project. This legal firm had an issue connecting a telephone enquiry quickly to the right legal practitioner.

Target Process	**Answer the phone**
Problem	It took on average 2.4 call-backs before an enquirer made direct phone contact with the right legal practitioner with the expertise to help.
Solution	A simple decision tree was created for receptionists. Each call triggered a series of questions based on the caller's responses.
Benefit	Use of the decision tree resulted in the right legal practitioner being connected directly to the caller with only an occasional call-back. In addition, there was a significant up-tick in new work won because the potential client was able to obtain preliminary advice during their first call.

1-page Project Brief for an FPI Project

To make each FPI Project Brief as easy as possible for the Process Manager to complete within about 45 minutes, we provide a standard 1-page template as shown in Figure 36.

Fast Process Improvement Project Brief

Target Process i.e. Name of the process in a verb + noun format (e.g. Invoice the customer)

Raise a Purchase Order

Project Background

Process Intent:
Raise a Purchase Order in a timely manner

Process Start:
Requisition has been raised

Process End:
Purchase Order has been received by the supplier

Inputs:
Product specification; Quantity required; Delivery date

Outputs:
Approved Purchase Order containing the correct information

Available Measurement Data (if any):
Times when supplier reports (verbally) that the Purchase Order has been received

Immediate Customer:
Our Finance Department

Customer Expectations *i.e. what the customer generally expects of the process output:*	*Customer Perceptions* *i.e. what the customer generally thinks of the actual process output:*
Real time tracking of the Purchase order process	Manual process with excessive hand-offs means that tracking a Purchase Order during the raising process is difficult

Why we need to improve this process:

1. The process takes too long
2. We cannot respond quickly to supplier questions concerning availability of their Purchase Order
3. The information contained is not always accurate

Quarterly Process Objective

Reduce the Cycle Time of the 'Raise a Purchase Order' process

KPI Specification (#, $, %):	*KPI Target: (#, $, %)*
% reduction in Cycle Time	>50%

Project Logistics

Project Sponsor (Process Manager):	*Planning Workshop Facilitator:*	*Team Members:*
Harry Spicer	Mary Banner	Trevor Blight; Joan Backhaus; Phil Rider (Project Manager)

Arrangements for the 2-hour Planning Workshop plus subsequent team meetings:
Planning Workshop 3 October 2020 9am – 11am in Meeting Room 2; At discretion of the Project Manager, team meetings by remote or face-to-face every 1-2 weeks for 8 weeks, until project fully implemented with QA Wedge.

Figure 36: 1-page Project Brief template for an FPI Project

Case Study: Anitua Group – Exotic Blend of Strategy plus FPI Projects

One of our more memorable engagements took place on Lihir Island in Papua New Guinea (PNG). Lihir Island is located in PNG's New Ireland Province, about 700 km northeast of Port Moresby.

Newcrest (Lihir Gold Ltd) runs a rich gold mine at the north end of the island. Prior to the mine, Lihirians survived through subsistence agriculture, supplemented by a few cash crops and fish.

The island consists of five distinct volcanoes. The presence of hot springs shows persistent geothermal activity. The gold being mined on Lihir Island is in the heart of the youngest volcano, Luise Caldera. The water in the volcano is under pressure at 200°C.

The Anitua Group was originally set up in 1989 for the people of Lihir Island to participate in the Lihir Gold project, one of the world's largest gold mines. Shareholders include six clan groups from the Lihir Group of Islands, plus the local level government business arm. Today, the Anitua Group is one of the largest single suppliers of goods and services to Lihir Gold Ltd. The group is now focusing on expansion throughout PNG.

A key factor in the Group's success on the island of Lihir is its pool of diverse, highly trained, and experienced employees. Anitua Group's employees are local Lihirians plus national and expatriate managers.

There is no doubt that developing and managing successful organizations in remote locations requires a unique way of thinking:

- A way of thinking that embraces the local people, their cultures, and their environments.
- A way of thinking that empowers people with a shared vision, a sense of purpose, and a committed passion.

Anitua Group's thinking is driven not only by its goal of sustainable solutions, but also by its commitment to delivering world's best practice in servicing the people of Lihir, including those involved in running the Lihir gold mine.

In 2011 under the guidance of its CEO Colin Vale, the MBE approach was first applied to the Anitua Group as a whole, followed by each of its (then) nine diverse SME Business Units:

- Anitua Construction Services
- Anitua Hardware
- Anitua Mining Services
- Anitua Radial Drilling Services
- Anitua Security Services
- Anitua Supermarket
- Lihir Auto Services
- Lihir Business Services
- NCS Holdings

For the MBE consultant, Dr Rehn, this whole extended project was an eye-opener. He recalls a few incidents that occurred during his involvement:

"As part of orientation before starting my consulting assistance program for the Anitua Group, I was introduced to a local Lihirian Chief who escorted me around the island to visit the gold mine and other local sights. I was taken aback by the impact of the gold mine operation on the landscape. Due to the open-cut ore extraction, mounds of waste rock lay everywhere. A network of large diameter plastic tubes had been inserted into the ground in many places to relieve the hot underground water and air pressure to make ore extraction easier. Out of these tubes came continuous plumes of sulphur dioxide (SO_2). When it rains (which it does often,) the water naturally reacts with the SO_2 to create atmospheric sulphuric acid! The open cut mine workers therefore needed to have fresh clothes provided every few weeks due to the corrosion. The corrosive environment also had a devastating impact on the bodywork of vehicles over time. Even rugged Toyota four-wheel-drive vehicles had a short life. In contrast, in areas of the island untouched by mining operations, the environment was lush, tropical and punctuated by occasional villages of Lihirians living much as their ancestors would have."

"The topic of environmental controls on Lihir is apparently a sensitive and complex one. I understand that for PNG, mining is central to the whole economy, providing 25% of the country's foreign exchange. The sensitive issue is on what terms and at what cost."

"Shortly after I had finished several training sessions on how to plan and implement FPI Projects and had returned to Melbourne temporarily, I received a call from the CFO. He

asked me if it would be okay to run a couple of simultaneous FPI Projects within the Finance and Accounting team. Naturally, I said yes.

Nine weeks later, I asked him how these projects went. He replied that they went well but that he personally found the twice-over experience as Project Sponsor (i.e., the Process Manager) "very sobering". He said that as a highly qualified and experienced CFO ex-pat from Australia, he thought he knew how best to fix the two processes in question without the involvement of the small autonomous teams. However, he was impressed when he discovered that the two teams of Lihirians had come up with process fixes that were far better than he had envisioned. He said he was simply unaware of what the real problems were at the coalface and so had failed to envisage the right solutions."

"Unfortunately, in those days, safety controls were not high on the agenda. While on a site visit to the Lihir Gold Mine with the Management Team of Anitua Mining Services, we witnessed a drilling operation with an augur machine being operated by a small team of local employees, one of which was guiding the rotating augur into the hole with his bare hands. As the augur went deeper, a new augur extension of several meters would be bolted on. Unfazed by the protruding bolt heads at the join, the operator still used his bare hands to guide the rotating augur. Later, I met one of the operators who had lost two fingers while on the job. Needless to say, this drilling process was the subject of a subsequent FPI Project aimed at improving the safety of the operators."

"Things don't always go to plan on Lihir Island. After six new accommodation units had been built to house island visitors, the Australian ex-pat construction supervisor provided detailed instructions to the newly-appointed cleaning lady for the units in how to clean a toilet properly. To make sure that everything had been understood, he demonstrated the technique in Unit #1 and immediately asked the lady to repeat the process, which she did. A few days later he checked to see how things were going on site and was aghast to discover that only 1 of the 6 toilets had been cleaned. When he confronted the lady, she explained that he had shown her how to clean the toilet in Unit #1 but had said nothing about

how to clean the toilets in Units 2-6. His lesson: One has to be very specific when giving instructions in PNG!"

Anitua's current portfolio now includes 16 subsidiaries and employs 3,500 people in 30 locations throughout PNG and in Australia. In doing so, it has become an exemplary company in managing tribal complexities.

It is now 8 years since we introduced the full MBE approach into the Anitua Group. In September 2019, its founding CEO of 20 years, Colin Vale retired, and the new CEO John Gethin-Jones was appointed. John was previously the CEO of Anitua's largest subsidiary company, NCS Holdings. NCS Holdings is now the largest catering and camp management company in PNG. In commenting on his predecessor, John had this to say:

"Colin Vale took Anitua from a bunch of companies all working individually, with no synergies or group direction, to what is now considered the most successful landowner company in PNG."

"We are still focused on achieving the 'Lihir Destiny'— of being non-reliant on mining activities on Lihir, to ensure the future of all Lihirians."

"While the rate of return on investment (ROI) is a key indicator of the company's performance, the principles of business excellence play a large part in the company's planning."

"Anitua has 3-year strategic and business improvement plans for each of its 16 businesses, all sitting under a master 3-year strategic plan for the Group."

John Gethin-Jones, CEO Anitua Group

Case Study: Software Consulting Firm—FPI Project for a common problem

One of the biggest and most harmful weaknesses in business today is the lack of role clarity. A lack of clearly defined responsibility accompanies a lack of accountability. Important things will continually fall between the gaps because no one takes ownership.

During the strategic planning process of a software consulting client, it became clear that they had an issue with staff not completing timesheets accurately and on time. This was a real problem, because as a service-based consulting business, they sell the time spent on their contracted projects. Therefore, timesheets are of vital importance. Their people focused on supplying excellent service to their clients and were not focused so much on the time taken to do so.

At month's-end, the office manager would ask for timesheets, and only then would the people try to figure out what projects they had worked on for that month. No-one was tracking their time as a matter of routine.

Consequently, they occasionally left significant amounts of income unclaimed by under-estimating the time worked on projects. At other times, they left themselves open to potential disputes with their clients by overestimating the time spent on their projects. On one occasion the firm was embarrassed when a client complained they had over-charged on a fixed-price purchase order by several hundred dollars. They also had instances where they were three weeks late invoicing their clients because their timesheets were not in order. This created cash flow issues for the business.

We facilitated a standard 2-hour FPI Planning Workshop, aimed at solving the timesheet problem permanently.

The first thing they did post-workshop was to hold a company-wide meeting and explain why timesheets were important, and how and when they needed to be filled out. Now, a weekly email goes around every Monday morning, reinforcing why sending accurate timesheets on time is valuable. That email includes a list of people who haven't submitted the timesheets for the previous week by 10 am on the following Monday.

Interestingly, the worst culprits for not completing timesheets properly had been the senior managers. They quickly agreed to lead from the front on this. Within a month of the FPI Planning Workshop,100% of timesheets were received on time.

The new timesheet process also clarifies when and how to fill in the timesheets during the week.

Some employees had previously been unclear on which types of work were chargeable, and how to categorize them. They realized they were consistently underestimating design time, and therefore undercharging. That meant they were constantly going over budget on contracted projects. They can now review how much time is being spent in different aspects of each project and allow for appropriately flexible resource allocations on the longer-term projects.

The outcomes of this FPI Project were two-fold:

1. They have confidence they're filling in the right information and therefore invoicing correctly.

2. The company's office manager no longer spends one week every month chasing people's timesheets and dealing with issues related to poor accuracy. This saved 40 hours of effort per month.

And to highlight the fact that even business excellence experts are not immune to these kinds of issues, Dr Rehn admits that when he ran his own management consulting company, they had exactly the same issue. Guess who was the worst at entering timesheets on time—Dr Rehn!

Business Process Reengineering Projects

It is not enough to do lots of top-down and bottom-up FPI Projects for the business. If occasional top-down, end-to-end reengineering of your Key Business Processes is not done well, your business performance will always be sub-optimal.

A BPR Project is triggered whenever the Management Team believes it's time for fundamental improvement in any one of its Key Business Processes. A BPR Project may also be triggered in response to Opportunities or Threats that surface during strategic planning, or when there is a perceived need to embrace technological change.

Since every Key Business Process is highly significant for the well-being of the business, fundamental reengineering will generate big positive implications for your business. Your BPR Project priorities and their proposed timing over the planning period should therefore be indicated clearly on your 1-page Process Model and brought forward to form one Objective of your 1-page Strategic Plan.

2-day BPR Planning Workshop

On Day 1 of our standard 2-day BPR Planning Workshop, the existing Key Business Process is mapped to both clarify and heavily critique the current "AS IS" process. On Day 2, the "SHOULD BE" version of the Key Business Process is developed from scratch. The redesigned process must fix all the problems identified on the previous day for the AS IS process. The impact of any new software and its planned interaction with the process participants and their new roles is modelled as part of the SHOULD BE version.

Note: The "AS IS" and "SHOULD BE" processes are mapped using a swim lane flow diagram. Where the different actors (roles and software systems) get a lane to visualize their involvement in the process. Please see Appendix A: Further Resources for further details on how this can be run.

At the end of the two days, you'll not only have an updated process design, but you'll also have a detailed Action Plan to shift from the current damaged process to the new improved process.

During the Planning Workshop, accountable Team Leaders are selected for every action of the implementation Action Plan and those actions are scheduled. A well-planned implementation of the Action Plan for a BPR Project typically takes 3-18 months to complete, depending on the scope of the SHOULD BE specification.

Reflecting its strategic importance, progress is reviewed by the Management Team at the Progress Review Meeting every month.

Unlocking Massive Net Benefits through BPR Projects

Process reengineering involves completely redesigning and building a targeted Key Business Process from the ground up. It often requires implementation of a major new software platform such as Customer Relationship Management (CRM) or Enterprise Resource Planning (ERP).

> *"ERP platforms are the most in-demand software for small businesses, next to business management and marketing technology."*[30]

> *"Owners of SMBs prefer using ERP systems instead of standalone solutions because it can reduce operation costs by*

> *11%, standardize back-office processes by 77%, and give them real-time visibility into their data by 48%."*[30]

Despite the popularity of ERP, the failure rate of ERP implementation remains high. Here are some recent statistics about ERP implementation problems[31]. They highlight the importance of getting it right the first time.

- *"80% of customers are unhappy with their current ERP*
- *60% of ERP projects fail*
- *57% of ERP systems take longer than expected*
- *54% of ERP systems exceed projected budget targets*
- *40% of ERP systems experience at-large operational disruption*
- *41% of enterprises fail to achieve more than half of the expected benefits"*

Case Study: B&R Enclosures – use of the BPR technique to specify requirements for a new ERP system

As its name implies, B&R Enclosures designs and manufactures enclosures. Robust enclosures are provided for the domestic, industrial, mining, oil and gas, energy, hazardous location and infrastructure market segments in Australia.

Back in 2012, the technology platform of B&R's ERP system had reached 'end of life'. After 20 years, it was time to modernize the business information system in order to support the company's strategic Objectives and achieve scalable growth.

The thought of changing over its ERP system had been daunting. While full of opportunity, the task represented a serious business risk. There were many stories of others who had taken on the challenge and had lost customers and momentum. And, it seemed, the ERP upgrade had failed to deliver on the benefits promised[31].

To clarify the detailed operational requirements of a mooted new ERP system, a representative team of B&R key personnel applied the MBE methodology for BPR to two consecutive Key Business Processes of the business:

1. Bring in the Order
2. Fulfill the Order

Each required a standard 2-day BPR Planning Workshop of the appropriate participants. The dual intent for the redesigned process combination was to:

- Reduce the Cycle Times by 50% and reduce the Lead Times by 50% in all areas
- Develop a 'Performance Specification' for the proposed new ERP system that could be used to test and choose the new ERP system vendor within 3 months of the two BPR Planning Workshops

This was the first time the MBE team had used our 2-day BPR planning technique to develop a customized Performance Specification for a mooted large IT system. B&R went on to shortlist two vendors, issue Request-For-Tenders (RFTs) to these two vendors, and then choose the preferred one.

> *"The BPR technique enabled us to create and focus on a vision of operational excellence that has been the foundation element in our digital transformation strategy. B&R Enclosures has just received an Award by its ERP vendor for its exemplary implementation."*
>
> Chris Bridges-Taylor, Director and General Manager B&R Enclosures

1-page Project Brief for a BPR Project

To make each BPR Project Brief as easy as possible for the Process Manager to complete in about 60 minutes, we provide a standard 1-page template as shown in Figure 37.

You can see that our 1-page template for this Brief has the *same* format as the one for an FPI Project (refer Figure 36). However, given the high stakes associated with every BPR Project, the Process Manager should take special care in crafting this type of Brief.

The completed Brief should then be approved by the full Management Team and then issued to all the nominated participants for the 2-day BPR Planning Workshop.

Business Process Reengineering Project Brief

Target Process i.e. Name of the process in a verb + noun format (e.g. Win a job)
Position the business in the marketplace

Project Background	
Process Intent: Ensure the right marketing messages are conveyed to the right market segments at the right time	
Process Start: With the notable exception of marketing materials and approaches, we have successfully integrated the recent company acquisition	
Process End: All online and other marketing messages and channels have been redesigned to cater for our new combined range of product and service offerings	
Inputs: Forecasts for product demand; Historical sales data; Profitability by product; List of current customers	
Outputs: Published marketing messages to target audiences	
Available Measurement Data (if any): Number of potential customers registering online per month with their email address	
Immediate Customer: Target audiences	
Customer Expectations *i.e. what the customer generally expects of the process output:* To be fully aware of what we can do for them and to be excited at the prospect	*Customer Perceptions* *I.e. what the customer generally thinks of the actual process output:* Our online messaging is poor; Our brochures all need updating for content and appearance
Why we need to improve this process: 1. Integrating our acquired competitor has entailed a lot of effort and in the meantime, our Sales revenue has dropped steadily – large due to our decreased efforts devoted to marketing and sales 2. We are receiving a lot of negative customer feedback regarding the tired look of our printed materials and slide presentations	

Project KPI	
KPI Specification (#, $, %): % increase in annual Sales from end 2019 to end 2020	*KPI Target: (#, $, %)* > 20%

Project Logistics		
Project Sponsor (Process Manager): Peter Jensen	*Planning Workshop Facilitator:* Jack Thomas	*Team Members:* Jenny Samson, Jill Edwards, Rex Svenson, Spencer Liston, Lorraine Cox, Richard Rollins, Henry Jones, Trevor Black (Project Manager)
Arrangements for the 2-day Planning Workshop plus subsequent team meetings: Planning Workshop 6-7 December 2020 8.30am – 5.30pm in Meeting Room 1; At discretion of the Project Manager, team meetings by remote or face-to-face every 2 or 4 weeks until project fully implemented with QA Wedge.		

Figure 37: 1-page Project Brief template for a BPR Project

Common Planning Methodology for Both FPI and BPR Projects

Having just described the nature and intent of FPI Projects and BPR Projects for improving your repetitive processes, it's time now to explain the common methodology that should be applied during their respective 2-hour and 2-day Planning Workshops.

As foreshadowed earlier in this book, we adapt a simplified version of the methodology invented by Walter Shewhart in 1926 and subsequently popularized by the quality guru, Edwards Deming in the 1950s.

The "PCDA Wheel + Wedge" Process Improvement Technique

The Shewhart PDCA methodology can be applied to *any* process that is repetitive. Remember that this technique should NOT be applied to any process that is *non*-repetitive (e.g., Close the factory in Alabama). For such once-only processes, the traditional Project Management methodology is the most appropriate to use for process execution and delivery.

A huge handicap for most SMEs is that they are not aware of the power of the Shewhart standard process improvement methodology. Consequently, they apply Project Management by default in trying to fix *every* problem in the organization—*including those problems that relate to repetitive processes.* Given the reality that approximately 95% of the average employee's work involves *repetitive* processes, applying Project Management techniques to solve these process problems is problematical. To begin with, employee effort is far greater than it would be if the right process improvement techniques were applied. Furthermore, some of the Root Causes of process problems are not identified and therefore not redressed by project management techniques.

Applying the wrong process improvement technique when trying to improve any of the 95% of work processes is grossly sub-optimal.

And to make matters worse, the results are usually temporary.

Figure 38: World class businesses don't make this mistake, and neither should you

The big difference between standard Project Management, and Fast Process Improvement is the linear versus circular, iterative nature:

- With Project Management, you're only going to do something once, and so the emphasis is on getting things done in the right linear sequence to meet a deadline.
- Process Improvement is a circular, iterative technique designed to deliver permanent process improvements with the minimum possible effort.

The PDCA process improvement methodology should be used whenever a repetitive process is not performing well and more than one person needs to be involved in reaching an agreeable solution.

The people *directly involved* in executing the process should be involved in developing the solution. In addition, there are times when it may be ideal to include people indirectly involved in the process. Depending on the circumstances, it may also be wise to include an internal or external customer representative for broadened insight into the process problems and potential solutions.

The size and importance of the targeted process determines the number of people on the improvement team. Teams may have 3 to 8 members. In general, the larger the targeted process, the larger the team needs to be for proper representation of the process participants.

The method for improving the process involves simple, structured techniques to quickly identify the Root Causes of undesirable process variations. *Variation is the disease of all repetitive processes.* Before the improvement team disbands, the Root Causes of unwanted process variation should be fixed permanently.

Figure 39 illustrates the essence of this methodology.

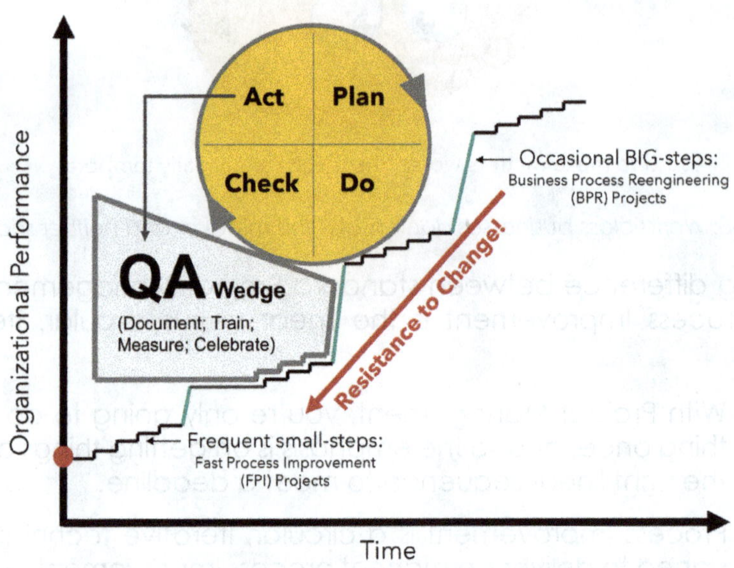

Figure 39: The Shewhart PDCA team-based methodology for improving repetitive processes

Metaphorically speaking, to permanently raise operational performance over time in either small or big steps, two ingredients are needed:

1. A "Wheel of Progress" (PDCA Cycle) capable of being pushed uphill by the Process Improvement Team one notch at a time against the gravity of resistance to change.

2. A "Wedge" (referred to as Quality Assurance or QA for short) which constitutes everything the organization must do to guarantee that this improved process will never again be done the old way.

Note: This means that QA must include the minimum necessary effective documentation (stored in the organization's Quality Management System or QMS,) transition training, transition measurement, and celebration of the Project results. Any more than the *minimum necessary* would add waste to the new process.

Note: The team must not disband until it has put in place all the necessary QA. Otherwise, a dangerous "hand-off" would be created if the team tried to delegate QA to some central person or group ostensibly "responsible for QA" or "responsible for Quality". Guidelines and coaching for how this should be done consistently by teams will be provided by the Process Manager of "Design and improve processes" plus "Capture and leverage knowledge".

The reason for including celebration as the fourth and final element of QA is that all employees need to see that your business really does value their process improvement efforts. Celebrating success is an important part of maintaining momentum.

With reference to Figure 38, the key driving idea behind process improvement is to repeatedly "Go up a notch—and whack in the QA Wedge to sustain the improvement."

Your QMS will contain the aggregated QA documentation and associated "how to" knowledge for all the organization's processes.

With reference to Figure 38, clearly Wheel without Wedge is a sub-optimal way to operate, as is Wedge without Wheel. Unfortunately, the world has far too many organizations at either end of this spectrum.

Based on our experience, we estimate that only about 1 in 20 businesses have the Wheel and Wedge working in total harmony—and understand their synergy for creating operational excellence. Is your business already one of those?

Case Study: Credit Union Australia (CUA)—Power of the QA Wedge

CUA is currently the largest credit union in Australia with 50+ Branches serving 500,000 members. It has over 1,000 employees.

In 2008, CUA adopted the MBE approach to formulation and execution of its national strategy, plus continuous process improvement.

In 2009, CUA scheduled and conducted 22 training sessions across its branch networks in Queensland, New South Wales, and Victoria for how best to undertake local continuous process improvements.

The intent was to have the trained employees undertake a raft of bottom-up small process improvement projects but not to have any projects duplicated across the network.

By doing things that way, each process improvement effected in one branch could be made permanent by applying the QA Wedge locally. However, here's the really important point: the techniques learned could then be leveraged quickly across all other 49 or so branches. This multiplier effect of the QA Wedge made the process improvement program outstandingly effective as the business progressively moved to standardize on the same best practice techniques across all Branches.

Years earlier, this same concept was made famous by the global McDonalds fast food franchise. In every McDonalds franchise operation, key processes were standardized so that the resultant food products and associated customer service were consistent. An improvement identified in one store was applied in the other stores.

Role of QMS and ISO 9001:2015

Obviously, it makes sense to employ as much *standardization* as reasonable in the way each individual process improvement team implements their QA upon completion of their project— until the process in question is due for further improvement.

This is why the world's Standards Associations entered the arena decades ago to suggest how a QMS might best be developed and maintained. The latest version of the world-wide QMS standard is known as ISO 9001:2015[32]. It sets out the implementation criteria for a QMS and any business may be certified as conforming to these criteria. The standard is based on a number of quality management principles including customer focus, the motivation and accountability of top management, the process approach and continuous improvement. The intent is to ensure that business customers receive products and services that meet a certain level of quality.

According to the International Organization for Standardization (ISO), there are over one million companies in over 170 countries which are currently certified to ISO 9001:2015. Given that there are

33 million SMBs in the US alone, the penetration of ISO certification in the SME / SMB sector worldwide is clearly very low.

The good news is that should you decide to obtain ISO certification of your QMS while you are implementing the MBE approach, your current practice will already be consistent with the ISO criteria. However, you would need to undertake an online course or engage a specialist consultant (not MBE) to formalize its alignment with the Sections of the ISO QMS Manual. You would also need to make arrangements for regular audits of your QMS system.

It's up to you to decide if the benefits of ISO certification will outweigh the costs of obtaining and maintaining it.

QA and Maintaining the QMS—Everybody's Job

Participating in QA is everybody's job (including a CEO) and contrary to widespread belief, cannot be delegated to some central person or organization "responsible for QA." However, it *is* okay to have a central QMS enabled by sound technology, And as we saw earlier, it is also okay to have a central person (i.e., the designated Process Manager for "Design and improve processes" plus "Capture and leverage knowledge") looking after the integrity of the system.

What is not acceptable is for a process improvement team to abdicate its responsibility for updating the central QMS to ensure that the new way of doing things becomes permanent and accessible. It is only by keeping the system updated that a new or existing employee can access the QMS to understand the latest instructions and guidance.

How the PDCA Cycle Works

The Wheel of Progress (i.e., PDCA Cycle) is based on common sense. That's why it's so successful and widespread. Here's how it works:

1. If you want to design or improve a process, you need to Plan it.

2. Then you need to Do (Test) it—i.e., execute the Plan—but usually as an experiment, not at full scale, because your Plan might be deficient in some way.

3. Next, you need to Check (by measuring before and after) to see if your experiment was successful.

4. Finally, if the Check proves positive, you make a note to Act, to "Wedge" the variable(s) you changed. Then you go back to the Plan quadrant of the PDCA Cycle to make further improvements (if considered necessary). On the other hand, if the experiment fails, you would bypass the Act quadrant altogether (apart from capturing what was learned) and begin the next cycle in the Plan quadrant.

The idea is to go around this PDCA Cycle one or more times until you've made major improvements to the targeted process. When you think you've gone far enough, you finish the Project by "Wedging" all the improvements you noted along the way.

However, the great news is that going around the PDCA Cycle only *once* is always enough to bring about a significant process improvement. The aim is to get progress quickly—not to get perfection slowly. If a process improvement team labors the point by going around the PDCA Cycle multiple times before inserting the QA Wedge, the team members become tired and their effectiveness declines.

Based on our experience over many years, we recommend that Fast Process Improvement (FPI) Projects should be time-boxed at no more than eight weeks' total duration. The implied assumption is that the team goes around the PDCA Cycle only once during this time.

By enabling FPI Projects to be instigated and completed within eight weeks, they can be undertaken readily within the quarterly cycle. Each quarterly cycle will include a premeditated mix of...

1. Top-down FPI Projects to deploy strategic Objectives down and across the organization,

   plus

2. Bottom-up FPI Projects to address employee process improvement suggestions.

The Plan (P) step is best done at a workshop involving a full-time team of the process participants. You literally cannot afford to have a critical process remain broken while your people engage in an extended part-time planning effort. Orchestration of part-time team planning efforts would also send the wrong message to employees about the importance of Process Design & Improvement.

The times required for the FPI and BPR Planning Workshops are short:

- Each FPI Project is planned in 2 hours
- Each BPR Project is planned in 2 days

Good facilitation skills are necessary to help each team stay focused on the task and to encourage healthy team dynamics.

Note: Further information on facilitation can be found in Appendix A: Further Resources.

Detailed Breakdown of the PDCA Cycle

A more detailed breakdown of the PDCA Cycle is presented in Figure 40, illustrating once again how simple this process is—so simple that anyone can participate, even a CEO.

The magic occurs at Step 3, because this is where the Root Causes of unwanted process variation are identified.

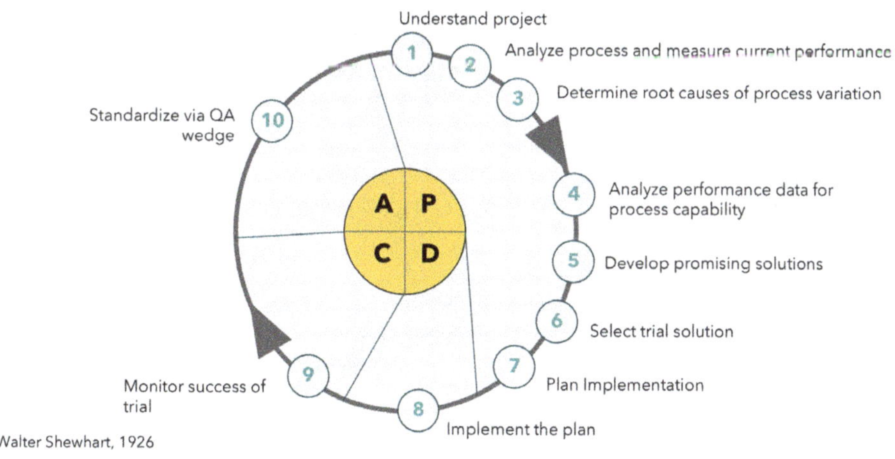

Figure 40: Detailed Breakdown of the PDCA Cycle

The potential role of technology in process improvement demands that the team undertake a technology scan during the project planning, specifically at Step 5 of the PDCA Cycle. Whereas business needs normally drive the demand for information technology, awareness of available information technology options can also enable a team to envisage exciting new ways of executing the process.

As the Project Sponsor for all proposed FPI and BPR projects, it is the Process Manager's responsibility to prepare a Project Brief for each one. The Project Brief helps the team avoid wasting precious time when convened for the corresponding 2-hour or 2-day Planning Workshop. By following the PDCA Cycle with clear "terms of reference", the team can also begin its planning work immediately.

Leveraging Knowledge through a Graphical QMS

It is imperative that the business keeps its entire process collection up to date every month. This is the collective responsibility of the Process Managers for all the Key Processes depicted in the 1-page Process Model.

The up-to-date process collection becomes the core of the organization's ever-improving QMS—i.e., the reference system for anyone within the business who needs to know how things should best be done for any Key Process or sub-process.

Knowledge hyperlinks should be added to individual process steps in your QMS. For example, you might append an explanatory video to the step: "Grease the vehicle." By this means, the company's process flows and knowledge flows become intimately linked. The business will be more efficient because every employee will know precisely what to do when executing their repetitive processes the best-known way.

The QMS should be structured to reflect the organization's process hierarchy, from Key (Level 1) Processes at the top, to their agreed sub-processes at Levels 2,3,4,5 and below if further documented detail is considered necessary. Employees can then access their desired level of detail on demand by clicking down through the process hierarchy.

As frequent FPI Projects and occasional BPR Projects continue to be executed, substantial benefits will be realized by having a QMS that reflects the collective ideas of all employees on best practice process and knowledge flows tailored to the nature and scale of the business.

Reminder: It is crucial to apply the QA Wedge (i.e., Document; Train; Measure; Celebrate) during the execution of every individual FPI Project and BPR Project. Not to do so would result in temporary process improvements rather than the desired permanent process improvements. You'll end up wasting the effort and run the risk of falling back to where you started.

Software Requirements for a Quality Management System (QMS)

When implementing a successful QMS for a small to medium business, the focus should be on the requirements that make the biggest difference. Many SMEs have limited IT capability so the system must be simple to set-up and maintain.

Here are some core requirements to assist you with assessing potential IT software for your QMS:

1. Provide a hierarchical structure to support desired levels of process detail, from the Level 1 Key Processes at the top right down to Level 6 sub-processes (if such fine detail is needed). Hierarchies are intuitive to a user. They provide a convenient way of starting with a high-level view (i.e., the 1-page Process Model) while enabling greater details to be viewed progressively as the employee digs deeper for more specific "how to" information.

2. Provide graphical representation of process steps using simple flow-chart icons.

3. Ensure that the information is online and can be easily accessed or edited by users with appropriate permission. A QMS will be used effectively when it is readily accessible, and users are confident it contains up-to-date information.

4. Remember that users will find it easier to consume the information if the layout is consistent. A well-known example of this is the *country* template for Wikipedia. The info-box is always on the right side and holds consistent information about each

country. There are also consistent headings for history, geography, government and politics, demographics, etc. This templated structure makes it easier for users to find what they're after faster and with less training.

5. Supply the capability to link and reference related information via hyperlinks, so users can follow them to find related information quickly.

6. Also remember that business knowledge is scattered across a variety of information media, such as Microsoft Office Excel files, Word files, plus sound and image files to name a few. The ability to embed, attach, and link to these files when needed ensures that all vital information is accessible within the QMS.

7. Enable employees to receive and respond to information requests from others within the business. The ability to share links to the proper information in the QMS reduces barriers to helping others and increases collaboration.

8. Supply high-level user control over searching for anything within the QMS. Sometimes it's too slow to click through the structured hierarchy when seeking the right piece of information. Similarly, general word searches are often not specific enough for efficient searching.

9. Make it possible to assign various permissions to different users (e.g., read-only permission; authoring permission; editing permission). This enables the QMS content to remain secure, relevant, and up to date.

Case Study: Abbott Vascular ANZ—Rapid Creation of a QMS

In 2007, Abbott Vascular ANZ's ROLE was defined as:

> *"We enhance the quality of patient care and health outcomes through advocacy and provision of minimally invasive vascular devices for Australia and New Zealand."*

What impressed us most about this client was their excitement and commitment regarding the need for immediate and strong process focus throughout their business.

Within a few weeks of completing their 2-day Foundation Planning Workshop, they had identified and agreed all Level 2 processes for each of their Key Business and Key Support Processes.

For example, the Level 2 processes for "Launch new products" were as follows:

- Enter product on New Product Launch Template
- Complete valuation model
- Obtain commercialization approval
- Establish demand forecast
- Produce and deliver launch kits
- Develop sales training program
- Train sales team
- Track post-launch activities

And for "Forecast demand for products and import stock," the Level 2 processes were:

- Review sales history of existing products
- Understand new product introductions and potential product obsolescence
- Determine any potential sales/market events that influence the forecast
- Review SKU / Item Number mix percentage vs. historical sales
- Submit Marketing Class Forecast by month
- Input and order stock from appropriate distribution center
- Analyze forecast accuracy vs. sales
- Analyze existing warehouse inventory and safety stock levels

And for "Design and improve processes," the Level 2 processes were:

- Establish common language and tools
- Train staff in process improvement tools and relevant techniques
- Identify broken or non-existent key processes and sub-processes

- Establish KPIs and reporting requirements for teams
- Assist Process Managers to develop KPIs and process improvement projects
- Facilitate the execution of process improvement projects
- Consult with teams and Process Managers regularly
- Celebrate process improvement successes

In total, Abbott Vascular ANZ had 16 Key Processes in their 1-page Process Model.

By being so quick off the mark, the framework was set for their QMS that would contain the details of how best to execute every Key Process of the entire business. Details of how to execute any repetitive process or sub-process of the business could be found by clicking their resultant process hierarchy down from any Key Process (i.e., at Level 1) down through its levels 2,3,4 etc. until the user's desired level of "how to" information had been reached.

This was of immense value for any new employee wishing to know how things should be done, and also for existing employees who needed to update their knowledge as a result of completed process improvement projects or job re-assignments.

Project Management Software

The well-known Project Management technique needs to be applied at many points along the MBE journey towards excellence and agility, in particular:

- Following each 2-hour Planning Workshop for a quarterly (or longer) Standard Project, when actions need to be executed within the scheduled timeframe
- Following each 2-hour FPI Planning Workshop, when actions need to be executed within the standard 8-week duration
- Following each 2-day BPR Planning Workshop, when actions need to be executed within the scheduled timeframe (i.e., 3-18 months)

Some basic requirements are listed below when assessing potential project management software for this purpose:

1. Ensure the software is easy to use so that employees who have never used project management software before can use it *intuitively*.
2. Supply templates for the three types of projects.
3. Enable attachments for supporting documentation.
4. Supply authorized online access to the project management software via a web browser.

Note: Some suggestions on the best tools to use for managing the different kinds of projects can be found in Appendix A: Further Resources.

Tracking Net Benefits of Completed FPI and BPR Projects Over Time

A major feature of the MBE approach is our simpler and extremely cost-effective technique for process improvements—much simpler and more cost-effective than Six Sigma. We strongly advocate fast quantification of the Net Savings achieved by every formal process improvement project, whether large or small.

Every year, your people will complete many FPI Projects and Standard Projects, but only 1-2 BPR Projects.

Upon completion of each FPI Project or BPR Project, quantification of the Net Savings can be done quickly and easily. The data are entered by the Project Manager upon project completion, and the software automatically calculates the Net Benefits and the Benefit to Cost ratio.

Many CEOs and managers are skeptical about the value of process improvement techniques—until they quantify and track the cumulative Net Benefits of completed projects. This is why we make it easy to keep track and report progress of all FPI and BPR Projects via a graphical summary of the quantified results.

After populating our standard 1-page Excel spreadsheet as each project is completed, it is easy to maintain a cumulative aggregate of the results across all projects from the beginning of the MBE implementation.

The Process Manager of the Key Support Process *Design and improve processes* should be responsible for adding the Benefits and Costs of each project to the cumulative Benefits and Costs of all completed process improvement projects to date. They maintain a live record of the overall impact of process improvements in your business and should be reported to the rest of the Management Team every month at the Progress Review Meeting.

This cumulative summary is depicted in Figure 41, where NPV stands for Net Present Value.

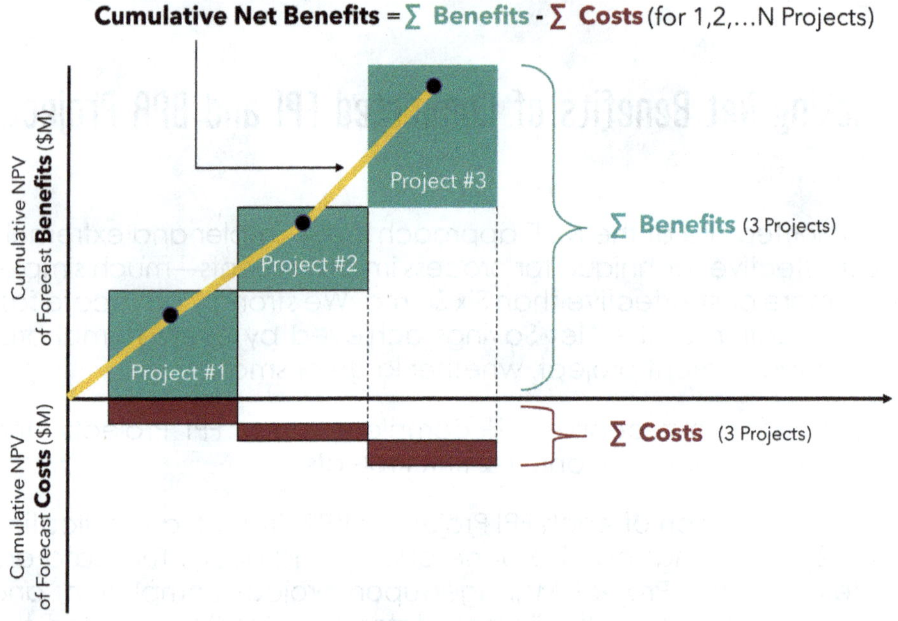

Figure 41: Tracking the financial net benefits of FPI and BPR projects

By accruing the Net Savings of these individual process improvement projects over time, you can compare the Annual Net Savings achieved by your people each year against the forecast cumulative Net Savings over 5 years of +22.5% of this year's (Year 0) annual Sales—as shown in Table 3.

Table 3: Forecast Annual Net Savings from continuous process improvement

Year 1	Year 2	Year 3	Year 4	Year 5
0.5% x Year 0 Sales	2.5% x Year 0 Sales	5.5% x Year 0 Sales	6.5% x Year 0 Sales	7.5% x Year 0 Sales

From a modest start in Year 1, your annual Net Savings will accelerate in Year 2 (the GROWTH Phase) and will continue to compound during Year 3 and beyond (the CONSOLIDATION Phase).

As you contemplate these results, please bear in mind that the predicted Net Savings are "Net" of all external and internal costs of the required ongoing implementation.

You will recall that there are two major sources of financial benefits from the pursuit of business excellence:

1. Net internal savings due to continuous process improvement
2. Top-line and bottom-line benefits due to increased sales revenue flowing from execution of the business strategy

The latter are difficult to forecast from historical case studies because they are so dependent upon the execution of each organization's unique Strategic Plan and associated marketing and sales strategies. Therefore, we make no attempt to do so.

The net internal savings due to continuous improvement alone will be enough to get everybody excited.

AFTERWORD

Now that you know why you might need My Business Excellence®, and how all the moving parts fit together, let's walk through the system. We're going to follow a case study from beginning to end. Then we'll wrap up with a few practical issues, such as getting the buy in from your Management Team, crossing the chasm between planning and execution, before ending, as all major achievements should, with celebration.

In this section, we're talking about how to implement MBE from the CEO's high-level perspective. Because the system and specific tools are ever evolving, we focus on the principles behind practical implementation rather than the minutiae.

First, let's look at how SMEs of varying size might handle implementation of the MBE approach differently.

10-49 Full-Time Employees (Small Enterprise):

1. Develop the 1-page Process Model and assign all Process Manager roles to at least 3 key people (including the CEO).
2. Ignore the potential role of BPR projects until Year 2 (i.e., after the fundamentals of the approach have been embedded in Year 1)
3. Develop the 1-page Strategic Plan for the chosen planning period, with the following single Objective in the Process layer of the Balanced Scorecard: "Deploy this Strategic Plan via quarterly FPI Projects and Standard Projects."
4. Include the following Objective in the People & Infrastructure layer of the 1-Year Strategic Plan: "Train all our employees in the Fast Process Improvement technique."
5. At each quarterly Planning Meeting of the Management Team, nominate at least one top-down quarterly Project for

strategy deployment—to be implemented by a small autonomous team. Nominate other bottom-up quarterly Project(s) for operational improvement, provided the business can resource it / them during the quarter.

6. Monitor the performance monthly against each quarterly Project.
7. At each quarterly Planning Meeting, maintain the currency of the 1-page Process Model and the1-page Strategic Plan, while tracking the KPIs for each Objective and for each Key Process.
8. Via a 1-day Strategic Planning Workshop, roll forward the Strategic Plan by 12 months at the end of each year.

50-500 Full-Time Employees (Medium Enterprise)

1. Develop the 1-page Process Model and assign all Process Manager roles to the Management Team members to best utilize their inherent expertise.
2. Prioritize one or at most two BPR Projects to be completed during Year 1 plus one or at most two BPR Projects for each of Years 2 and 3—the latter if the agreed planning time period is 2 or 3 years.
3. Develop the 1-page Strategic Plan for 1,3 or 5 years, with the adopted planning time horizon dependent on the perceived rate of change in the associated industry.
4. Include the pre-determined BPR priorities in the Process Objective of the 1-page Strategic Plan
5. At each quarterly Planning Meeting of the Management Team, have each Process Manager nominate their perceived highest priority projects and associated KPIs for the immediate quarter.
6. At this same meeting, then decide which quarterly Projects can be resourced across the business such that no employee is asked to take part part-time in more than one Project.

7. Monitor the performance monthly against each agreed quarterly Project and its KPI.
8. Maintain the currency of the Strategic Plan and Process Model every quarter, while tracking the KPIs for each Objective and for each Key Process.
9. Via a 1-day Strategic Planning Workshop, roll forward the Strategic Plan by 12 months at the end of each year.

Taking Your People with You

Implementing the MBE approach is itself a process. If you alone handle implementation as the CEO, it will fail. If you want it to work, you must enlist the active support of internal Process Managers and Project Managers who will join you in driving the necessary changes.

Case Study: Intrepid Travel and Intrepid Group

Intrepid Travel was co-founded in 1989 by two travelling friends Darrell Wade and Geoff Manchester. Their idea was to become something more than just a travel company by featuring travel "the local way" for more authentic traveler experiences—using local accommodation and transport; eating in local restaurants; travelling with local tour leaders.

From just 46 international travelers in their first year, annual sales revenue had grown steadily to $60M by 2005.

In 2005, we were brought in to help the business become a scalable, world class operation via the MBE approach. The Management Team wanted to combine Strategic excellence and Operational excellence.

Figure 42 shows their original Process Model developed during the 2-day Foundation Planning Workshop:

Our ROLE *(Level 0 process)*

We create interactive travel experiences globally to enrich peoples' lives.

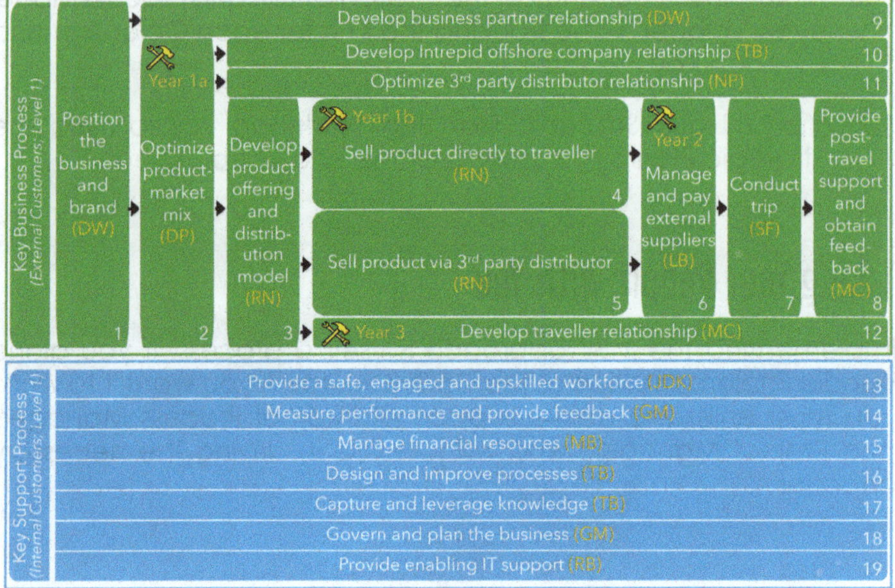

Figure 42: Intrepid Travel's original 1-page Process Model

The Process Model was used to target and then deliver the BPR priorities shown. In addition, the nominated Process Managers were responsible for sponsoring FPI Projects within their assigned Key Processes. All BPR and FPI Projects were delivered by small autonomous teams.

The BPR priorities highlighted in Figure 42 were automatically reflected in the company's 3-year Strategic Plan as in Figure 43:

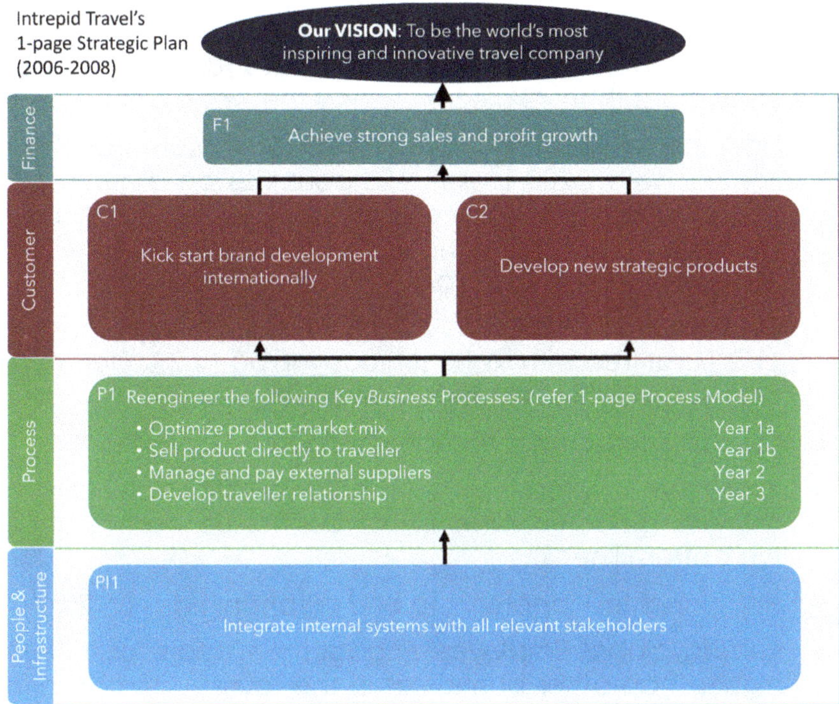

Figure 43: Intrepid Travel's 1-page Strategic Plan (2006-2008)

The company quickly became self-sufficient in applying the MBE techniques.

Here is what Darrell Wade had to say about the approach years later in 2012:

> *"It was big, grunty stuff and was part of the scaling that has helped the business go forward (from 500 travelers per annum to 350,000). It has completely changed the way we do things at Intrepid and we are a far more efficient, profitable company as a result. And less stressed!"*

Darrell Wade, Co-founder, Intrepid Travel and CEO PEAK Adventure Travel Group

Fast forward a further 7 years to 2019, and the Intrepid Travel Group has gone from strength to strength. Expanded through organic growth plus acquisitions, the Intrepid Group remains independently owned by the two original founders of Intrepid Travel.

Here are a few highlights from the 2018 Annual Report[33]:

- Headquartered in Melbourne Australia; 1800 staff and leaders in more than 40 offices around the world
- Now the world's largest provider of adventure travel experiences, with 2,700 trips in 120 countries on all seven continents operated by the Group's four operator brands (Intrepid Travel; Peregrine Adventures; Urban Adventures; Adventure Tours Australia)
- Gross revenue $402M in 2018; EBIT $15M; Return on Equity 11%; Debt free with Net Cash position up 12.7%; Decrease in overheads 23% of departed revenue
- Dedicated to being an Agile business
- Achieved B Corp carbon-neutral certification, joining a growing global community of businesses looking beyond the bottom line
- First global tour operator to end elephant rides (in 2014)
- Record global Employee Engagement score of 82% (15% higher than other businesses in the tourism and hospitality industry) and a record customer feedback score of 4.7 out of 5 for the year
- Almost a quarter of the company's 2018 profits paid out in bonuses
- The not-for-profit Intrepid Foundation thus far raised $6M for over 100 local and international charities by matching traveler and staff donations dollar-for-dollar

In February 2019, the Intrepid Group was included in *Fast Company's* prestigious annual list of the World's Most Innovative Companies for 2019. Headquartered in New York City, Fast Company is published by Mansuento Ventures LLC and can be found online at www.fastcompany.com.

In reflecting on Intrepid Group's current and past performance, Darrell Wade said this:

> *"The work we did together back in 2005 is as relevant today as it was then—indeed that work really was the start of an ongoing commitment to continuous improvement of business processes and strategic planning. You might have noticed in our integrated report that we've had our EBIT line growing faster than revenue for 4 years in a row now. Given*

that revenue has been growing at double digit each year, it's an impressive performance."

Darrell Wade, Chairman of Intrepid Group

Maintaining Momentum

There is, of course, always the danger that you and your team develop a strategy that never gets implemented properly. Alternatively, it may tick along nicely for a while and then lose momentum as the next shiny object leads you astray. Both are examples of the infamous "Strategy to Execution Gap."

We introduced a travel client to the MBE approach 10 years ago. They recently told us they wanted to get started again, because the three years following their involvement had been the best years of the business. But when their original 3-year Strategic Plan expired, they ran out of steam. They hadn't followed through on the need to roll forward their Strategic Plan every year after its inauguration year.

So how do you stay motivated and maintain momentum?

Rigorous implementation of the MBE approach deals with this intrinsically to a large extent, but first, let's consider the basic law of momentum. In order to achieve and maintain momentum, you have to do two things:

1. Get started
2. Don't stop

The secret to getting started?

1. Give people a real sense of ownership of the approach and its positive impacts

2. Be prepared to go where the implementation process takes you

3. Start with the low-hanging fruit to generate fast, early results

And the secret to not stopping?

1. Don't get complacent

2. Embed the process of monthly and quarterly review meetings to maintain momentum
3. Choose Objectives, KPIs and quarterly Projects that really do matter
4. Quantify the cumulative net savings over time

Celebration

Congratulations! You have made it to the end of the MBE approach, in theory at least. Now, before you rush off to begin implementing it, we would offer some suggestions for simple, appropriate celebrations. Of course, if you already have a culture of celebration, you won't have any problem with this, but if you're stuck for ideas, here are a few:

One important thing to note: ALWAYS reward and celebrate people within work time. People have families, commitments, outside lives. Don't add to their burdens by expecting them to give up their free time, even if it is to be recognized and celebrated. A half day go-carting is so much more enjoyable when it's instead of work and not after it.

Celebrating the Little Things

When you're dealing with a small win, a small Project, or one of those Projects when it feels like the only real win is that you can say, "At least that's over," small gestures often mean the most.

- Take the team out for coffee
- Order in pizza
- Take the time to publicly thank and acknowledge participants in front of the rest of the business
- Hand out stickers, certificates, or other small rewards if they make sense in the context of your business

Celebrating the Bigger Things

Make the rewards commensurate with the effort involved and the net savings to the business. When your team completes a major BPR Project that will save the business millions, a handshake and a thank you card might not cut it.

- Time off for good behavior—sometimes the best way you can show your appreciation is just to give people time off with no strings attached.
- Entertainment rewards—those go-carting, paint-balling, and other team-building experiences can also make fun rewards; just remember to do them in work time.
- Travel trips don't have to be to work conventions or conferences; unencumbered travel trips can be excellent rewards for those momentous achievements.

Working in a small team as we do, our go-to celebration is a simple cup of coffee as we share our successes—like getting to the end of this book!

Where to from here?

Now that you have seen how the My Business Excellence® framework can improve business performance and generate massive net benefits, you have two basic options:

1. Do nothing. Put this book down, forget about its contents and carry on as you were before. This is the most expensive option.

2. Implement the approach and start on your journey towards excellence. You won't regret it!

Assuming you are contemplating going ahead, we recommend you spend some time looking through the extra information and links we've compiled in Appendix A: Further Resources. You can also find extra information to help you on our website mybusinessexcellence.com.

To your future business success!

Mark Rehn, Founder My Business Excellence®

Mark James, CEO My Business Excellence®

Web: https://mybusinessexcellence.com/

Email: hello@mybusinessexcellence.com

Phone: +61 1300 722 81

References

INTRODUCTION

1. European Commission n.d., *What is an SME?*, viewed 21 November 2019, <https://ec.europa.eu/growth/smes/business-friendly-environment/sme-definition_en/>

2. Six Sigma Daily n.d., *What is Six Sigma?*, viewed 21 November 2019, <https://www.sixsigmadaily.com/what-is-six-sigma/>

3. Australia. Bureau of Industry Economics 1992, *The National Industry Extension Service (NIES) and industry development / Bureau of Industry Economics BIE [Canberra]*, viewed 21 November 2019, <https://catalogue.nla.gov.au/Record/1022938>

PART 1: WHY MY BUSINESS EXCELLENCE?

4. Barrows, E, *What is Strategy Execution?*, American Management Association, 24 January 2019, viewed 21 November 2019, <https://www.amanet.org/articles/what-is-strategy-execution/>

5. Jansen, H, *94 Mind-Blowing Strategy Execution Stats*, 5 October 2016, viewed 21 November 2019, <https://boardview.io/blog/strategy-execution-stats/https://boardview.io/blog/strategy-execution-stats/>

6. International Organization for Standardization, *ISO 9000 Family – Quality Management*, viewed 21 November 2019, <https://www.iso.org/iso-9001-quality-management.html>

7. Six Sigma Daily n.d., *What is Six Sigma?*, viewed 21 November 2019, <https://www.sixsigmadaily.com/what-is-six-sigma/>

8. Manavue Inc., *The Lean Approach For Improving Performance And Optimizing Added Value*, viewed 21 November 2019, <http://manavue.ca/si_mve_a/Lean_Approach.html>

9. Agile Strategies, *Building Agility through OKRs,* viewed 21 November 2019, <https://agile-strategies.com/about/agile-okrs/>

10. Business Performance Improvement Resource, *Business Excellence Models,* Viewed 21 November 2019, <https://www.bpir.com/total-quality-management-business-excellence-models-bpir.com.html>

11. Rehn, M, *The Business Case for Business Excellence,* viewed 21 November 2019, <https://www.dropbox.com/s/j0cbhgw8v8io2ia/The%20Business%20Case%20for%20Business%20Excellence.pdf?dl=0>

12. Dan, A, *Kodak Failed By Asking The Wrong Marketing Question',* CMO Network, Forbes, viewed 21 November 2019, <https://www.forbes.com/sites/avidan/2012/01/23/kodak-failed-by-asking-the-wrong-marketing-question/#6768c4f03d47>

13. Bizmanualz.com, *What is The Cost Of Poor Quality?,* viewed 21 November 2019, <https://www.bizmanualz.com/improve-quality/what-is-the-cost-of-poor-quality.html>

14. Standards Australia (SAI Global) *AS 2561-2010: Guide to the determination and use of quality costs,* viewed 21 November 2019, <https://infostore.saiglobal.com/en-au/Standards/AS-2561-2010-124137_SAIG_AS_AS_274385/>

15. LeBow, I, LinkedIn, Why Business Transformation Efforts Fail - Part I: Climate, 23 May 2018, viewed 21 November 2019, <https://www.linkedin.com/pulse/why-business-transformation-efforts-fail-part-i-climate-ines-lebow/>

16. Collins, J, *Good To Great,* Harper Business, 2001

PART 2: WHAT IS MY BUSINESS EXCELLENCE?

17. McGee-Abe, J, *The 8 Deadly Lean Wastes – DOWNTIME,* 8 August 2015, viewed 21 November 2019, <https://www.processexcellencenetwork.com/business-transformation/articles/the-8-deadly-lean-wastes-downtime>

18. Van Vliet, V, Toolshero, *PDCA Cycle,* viewed 21 November 2019, <https://www.toolshero.com/problem-solving/pdca-cycle-deming/>

19. Fooks, J H, *PROFILES for PERFORMANCE – Total Quality Methods for Reducing Cycle Time*, Westinghouse Quality Series, Addison-Wesley Publishing Company, 1993

20. Rehn, M, *Cost-Time Profiling and its Implications for Service Organisations*, 15 November 2014, viewed 21 November 2019, <https://www.dropbox.com/s/h578rlx8kpz9a66/Cost-Time%20Profiling%20and%20its%20Implications%20for%20Service%20Organisations.pdf?dl=0>

21. Ranjan, S, POLYMER ACADEMY, 20 September 2017, viewed 21 November 2019, <https://polymeracademy.com/quality-management-system-qms/>

22. International Organization for Standardization, *ISO 9000 Family – Quality Management*, viewed 21 November 2019, <https://www.iso.org/iso-9001-quality-management.html>

23. Suryawanshi, Y, *Leading Change: Why 70% of transformation programs fail*, 18 February 2016, viewed 21 November 2019, <https://www.linkedin.com/pulse/leading-change-why-70-transformation-programs-fail-d-suryawanshi/>

24. Kaplan, R S, and Norton, D P, *Translating Strategy into Action - The BALANCED SCORECARD*, Harvard Business School Press, Boston Massachusetts, 1996

25. Kaplan, R S, and Norton, D P, *THE STRATEGY FOCUSED ORGANIZATION – How Balanced Scorecard companies thrive in the new business environment*, Harvard Business School Press, Boston Massachusetts, 2001

26. Lafley, A G and Martin, R L, *PLAYING TO WIN – How Strategy Really Works*, Harvard Business School Publishing, Boston Massachusetts, 2013

27. Porter, M E, *Competitive Strategy – Techniques for Analyzing Industries and Competitors*, New York: Free Press, 1980

28. Treacy M, and Wiersma, F, *The Discipline of Market Leaders*, Addison-Wesley, 1995

29. Mind Tools, *Customer Intimacy – Providing Lifetime Value To Your Customers*, viewed 21 November 2019, <https://www.mindtools.com/pages/article/customer-intimacy.htm>

PART 3: IMPLEMENTING MY BUSINESS EXCELLENCE

30. FinancesOnline, *63 Key ERP Statistics: 2019 Analysis of Trends, Data and Market Share,* viewed 21 November 2019, <https://financesonline.com/erp-statistics-analysis-of-trends-data-and-market-share/>

31. Carlton, R, *Ten ERP failure statistics that highlight the importance of getting it right first time round,* ERP FOCUS, 23 August 2017, viewed 21 November 2019, <https://www.erp-focus.com/ten-erp-failure-statistics.html>

32. International Organization for Standardization, *ISO 9000 Family – Quality Management,* viewed 21 November 2019, <https://www.iso.org/iso-9001-quality-management.html>

33. Intrepid Group, *ANNUAL REPORT 2018,* viewed 21 November 2019, <https://www.intrepidgroup.travel/sites/default/files/2019-04/IG_Annual_Report.pdf>

APPENDIX A: FURTHER RESOURCES

34. Santos, J M D, PM project-management.com, *Top 10 Best Project Management Software & Tools in 2019*, 5 October 2019, viewed 21 November 2019, https://project-management.com/top-10-project-management-software/?gclid=Cj0KCQiAiNnuBRD3ARIsAM8Kmls-tSbZbyvt4WI86UrJy6p_9lHVr_t5h2FWInlBDKtB-ENZLrZF91QaArlVEALw_wcB

Note: The web addresses referenced in this book were live and correct at the time of the book's publication but may be subject to change.

APPENDIX A: Further Resources

What Further Resources?

This appendix provides further instructions and links to external resources that will assist you in implementing the MBE approach in your business. A range of different instructional documents, templates and software we provide will make life easier.

Some of these resources are free while others are products and services for purchase at modest cost if you feel you need extra assistance.

Detailed Instructions and Supporting Templates

We have assembled a list of free supporting documents that we use regularly during our coaching engagements. These include:

- A presentation designed for briefing your Management Team on the MBE approach
- Detailed instructions on how to run FPI and BPR process improvement Projects
- Project Brief templates for Standard, FPI and BPR Projects
- An Agenda plus meeting-minute template for the monthly Progress Review Meetings
- An Agenda plus meeting-minute template for the quarterly Planning Meetings
- A spreadsheet that calculates the Net Benefits and Benefit : Cost ratio for every completed FPI or BPR Project

Over time, further documents will be added to this repository of free documents. You can access them at mybusinessexcellence.com/free-documents.

Capability Assessment Quiz

The Capability Assessment Quiz is an excellent way to get a baseline on how capable your business is in implementing business improvements right now. I can also be used to track your progress as you implement the MBE approach. The report that we generate from the quiz will highlight your strengths and weaknesses and provide recommendations on how best to take the next steps towards excellence.

You can access the quiz at mybusinessexcellence.com/capability-assessment-quiz.

MBE Platform

The MBE Platform underpins all the services we offer. Every business we work with has a business account that allows employees to track their progress as they move through the MBE implementation phases. As part of the MBE Platform, your employees can also access additional guides and software tools that will help them in their ongoing efforts to improve their business.

Find out more about the platform at mybusinessexcellence.com/platform.

Facilitation Guides

Facilitation is a critical element for the various workshops featured in our MBE approach. We take the guesswork out of how best to run each workshop by providing detailed, step-by-step guides to deliver each workshop perfectly within the prescribed time frames. These are the same facilitation guides we ourselves use when we facilitate the various MBE workshops for our clients.

Project Managing FPI, BPR and Standard Quarterly Projects

While there are numerous project management tools on the market that can be configured to administer the different kinds of projects required by our MBE approach. We recognize that many businesses don't have the time or resources to manage this process.

We have created turnkey project management software specifically designed to manage process improvement projects using the PDCA Cycle + Wedge outlined in our approach. Furthermore, this project management software can...

- Link each Project to its correct Key Process in your 1-page Process Model.
- Link the QA 'Wedge' documentation generated as part of each BPR and FPI Project to the internal process catalogue available within the MBE Platform (more on this below).
- Track the Net Benefits for each Project and accumulate them over time to track your return on investment while implementing the MBE approach.

1-page Process Model and 1-page Strategic Plan

Business Dashboards can be configured to show your 1-page Process Model and 1-Page Strategic Plan via your web browser. These dashboards become the nerve system of your monthly and quarterly reporting, with links allowing fast access to different aspects of your progress towards both Operational and Strategic excellence.

KPI Reporting

You can track all your KPIs from within the MBE Platform. Reviewing the health of your operations and progress towards your strategic Objectives with your Management Team is easy when your KPI data is available in graphical form that highlights emerging trends and triggers corrective action when needed. These reports for your company's high level KPIs are reviewed by the Management Team at each quarterly Planning Meeting.

The MBE platform also enables tracking of the KPIs for individual quarterly Projects. These reports are reviewed by the Management Team at each monthly Progress Review Meeting.

Quality Management System (QMS)–Process Catalogue and More

The MBE platform enables your people to progressively build your company's complete process catalogue in easy-to-navigate, hierarchical form. It also enables your people to link important reference documents (i.e., "how to" knowledge) to the relevant process steps at any level. Finally, our QMS functionality provides hot links to all current FPI and BPR Projects associated with each Key Process.

Alternative Software Tools

We advocate use of all the above software support tools because they are tailored to suit the MBE approach. However, you may decide instead to adapt a range of other software tools that you may be using already and augment these with other non-MBE software tools available in the marketplace.

Here are a few tips if you decide to do this…

Project Management[34]

Project management software helps Project managers and teams manage time, budget and scope constraints.

According to a recent survey done by Software Advice, about 46% of small enterprises are still using manual methods for organizing and tracking their projects. Given the large number of Projects implemented as part of the MBE approach, manual methods will be grossly inefficient–particularly for providing progress reports and sharing visibility.

Many SMEs are now using online project management software featuring cloud-based technology offered as Software-as-a-Service (SaaS).

Multiple software options are available and choosing the right one for your business can be confusing. Here are some of them…

- Monday.com
- Wrike
- Mavenlink

- Smartsheet
- Productive
- ProWorkflow
- Jira
- Quire
- AceProject
- Intervals
- Microsoft Project

Our advice? If you wish to acquire a third-party software offering for project management, choose the simplest possible one to manage all MBE Projects. These Projects do not require advanced project management features.

Please bear in mind that when taking the initiative to implement a project management tool throughout your business, not everyone is going to be happy. Your employees are already accustomed to doing things their own way, so causing any disruption may trigger some aversion. However, at the end of the day, the software will make their work easier. Make sure you have strong backing from the full Management Team before introducing it.

Knowledge Management System

When building a successful Knowledge Management System for an SME, the focus should be on the core requirements that make the biggest difference. Many businesses have limited IT capability and so the solution must be simple to set up and maintain.

Hierarchical Structure

A hierarchical structure is intuitive to a user and is a convenient way of starting with a high-level process view (i.e., 1-page Process Model) while enabling greater details and context to be reviewed progressively as people dig deeper for more specific information.

Live Documentation

It is vital that information is online and can be readily editable by authorized users. For a system to be used actively and effectively, it must be readily accessable and users must have confidence that it is up to date.

Information Templates for Different Kinds of Information

Users will find it easier to consume the information contained within the system if the layout of different types of information is consistent. A real-world example of this is the 'country' template for Wikipedia. The "infobox" which is always on the right-hand side contains consistent information about each country. There are also consistent headings for history, geography, government and politics, demographics etc.

Such a templated structure will make it easier for users to find what they're after faster and with less training.

Dynamic Linking

The ability to link and reference related information via hyperlinks allows users to "follow the bouncing ball" to find related information quickly.

Flexible Capture and Presentation of Differing Information Formats

The knowledge of a business is scattered through many different information media–different Microsoft Office® files, text files, video files, sounds and images to name a few. The ability to embed, attach and link to these files will ensure all important information is accessible within your Knowledge Management System.

Easy Sharing

Employees regularly receive information requests from others within the business. The ability to share a link to the appropriate information reduces the barriers to assisting others and so increases responsiveness.

Advanced Search Capability

Often just storing information hierarchically along process lines isn't enough. For an employee to use the knowledge base regularly, they must be able to find the proverbial 'needle in a haystack'. Being able to provide a high level of control over what the user is searching for, rather than just general word searches, is very important.

Role-Based User Access

Being able to add authorizations for creation, editing, read-only etc. to individual roles enables the content to remain secure, relevant and up to date.

Alternative Knowledge Management Software

- Microsoft Sharepoint
- Atlassian Confluence
- Mediawiki
- XSOL
- Bookstack

If the business has a large sunk investment in any of these or similar software platforms, consideration could be given to using one or more to build the Process Knowledge Database involving digital artefacts and the required graphical cascade of process flows and knowledge flows.

However, such a decision should not be taken lightly, since configuring a good Knowledge Management System or QMS from scratch to suit the MBE approach to business transformation is not a trivial undertaking.

Beanbag Training Kit for Fast Process Improvement

FPI Projects are central to improving all the Key Processes within your business. The most effective way of teaching the FPI methodology is via our Beanbag Training Kit. This kit includes all the equipment plus detailed instructions needed for how to run this fun, hands-on FPI training session for up to 12 people at a time–although extra people may attend the interactive session as spectators. Throwing the beanbags at a target is a process. The training session demonstrates how to find the top three root causes of the process variation, and then demonstrates how to "fix" these three root causes to get stunning results.

The techniques used in this session are exactly the same as those that will be needed to improve a "real world" work process. Following their participation in a beanbag training session, employees, including all members of the Management Team, will be ready and able to participate in subsequent real-world FPI Projects.

You can purchase a Beanbag Training Kit–complete with instructions on how to use it–from our website at mybusinessexcellence.com/fpi-training-kit.

BPR Planning Workshop Kit

BPR Planning Workshops involve two intense days for the designated team.

The "AS IS" version of the targeted Key Business Process is modelled and critiqued on day 1. The root causes of the process variation are the main deliverable from the Day 1 Activities.

On Day 2, the new optimized "SHOULD BE" process is modelled and specified in detail ready for follow-on implementation after the Workshop. Every one of the root causes identified on Day 1 are overcome by the SHOULD BE process design. We've found the most effective way of collaboratively working on a process isn't being crowded around a computer screen mapping out the processes. Instead, it's by working hands-on with "post it" notes and two large pieces of paper. How large? 1.2 meters wide and 6 meters long large!

The BPR Planning Workshop Kit includes 2 rolls of 6 meter-long heavy duty paper plus all the color-coded "post it" notes and permanent markers required to run the 2-day Planning Workshop session. The kit comes complete with an Agenda plus detailed instructions for getting everything done in the time allocated.

Further information and purchase instructions for the kit can be found at mybusinessexcellence.com/bpr-planning-kit.

Coaching, Training and Facilitation

While the MBE approach is methodical, logical and sequenced, it can still be challenging to stay on top of the implementation while also spending time working IN the business.

Many clients have realized a significant reduction in their required time input–plus a dramatic improvement in their forward momentum–when we are engaged to assist them in their phased MBE implementation. By engaging us, you have access to highly experienced professionals who live and breathe this approach day in and day out. We can provide...

- Coaching support for you and your Management Team
- Facilitation of all the different workshops and meetings, starting with the 2-day Foundation Planning Workshop in Phase 1
- Training for all employees in Fast Process Improvement

To find out more, please visit mybusinessexcellence.com and review our different engagement plans.

APPENDIX B: Examples of 1-page Process Models

Indicative 1-page Process Model for a Construction Business

Our ROLE *(Level 0 process)*
We provide design and construction services for process industry clients in Manitoba.

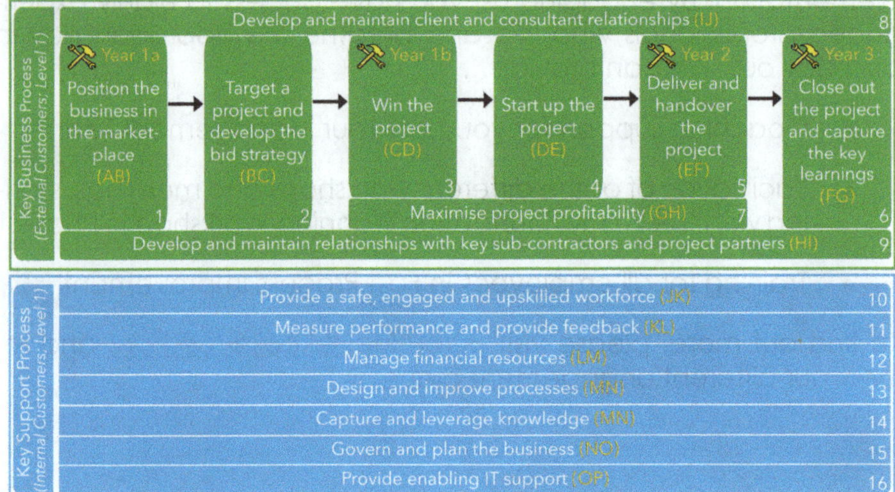

Indicative 1-page Process Model for a Legal Services Business

Our ROLE *(Level 0 process)*
We provide legal advisory services for public and private sector clients throughout the Mid West.

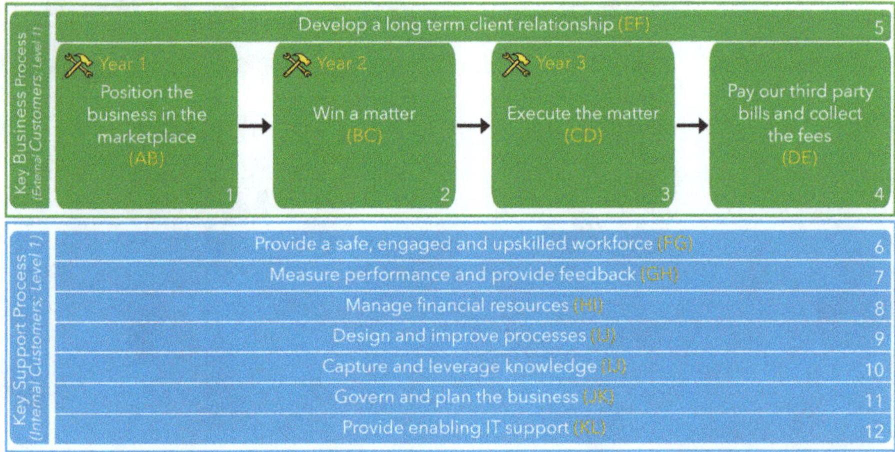

Indicative 1-page Process Model for a Public Transport Business

Our ROLE *(Level 0 process)*

We develop, build and operate a light rail network for city commuters.

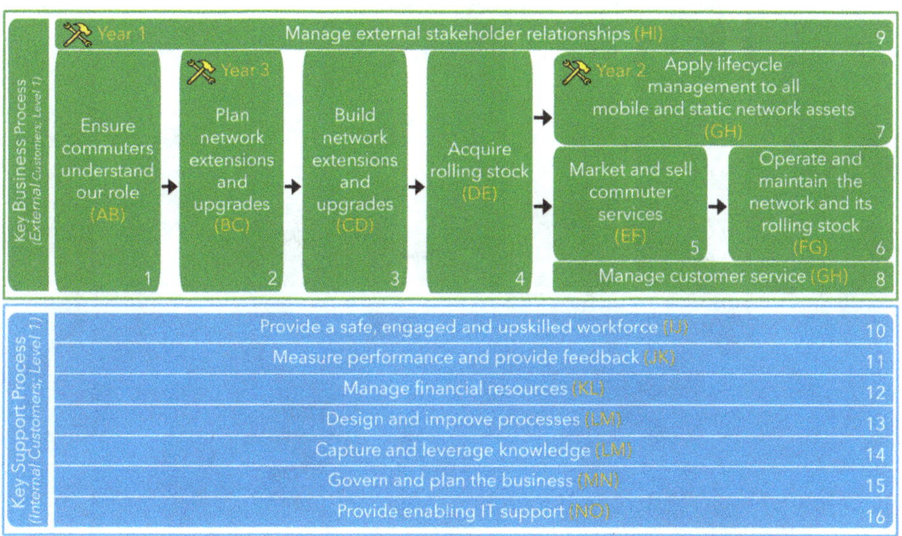

Indicative 1-page Process Model for a Research Business

Our ROLE *(Level 0 process)*

We provide horticultural research services in New Zealand, Australia and targeted overseas markets.

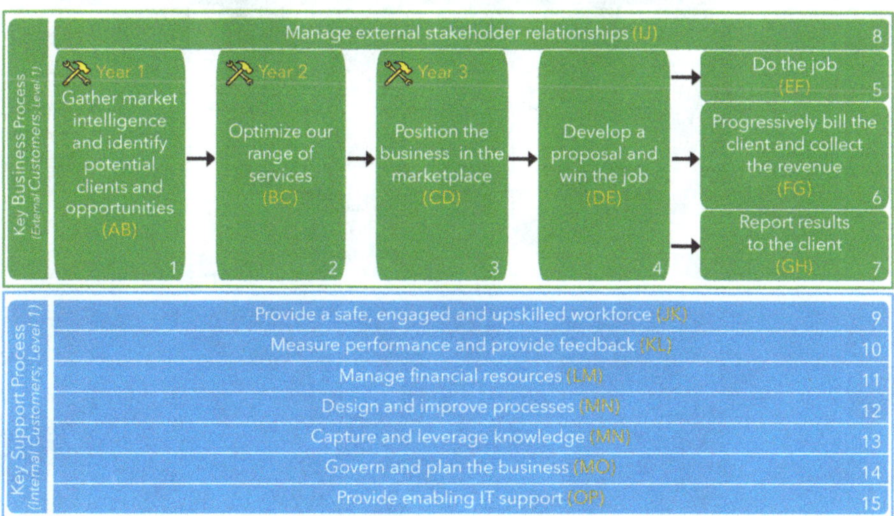

Indicative 1-page Process Model for a Retail Business

Our ROLE *(Level 0 process)*

We sell high end audio products to audiophiles in New Zealand.

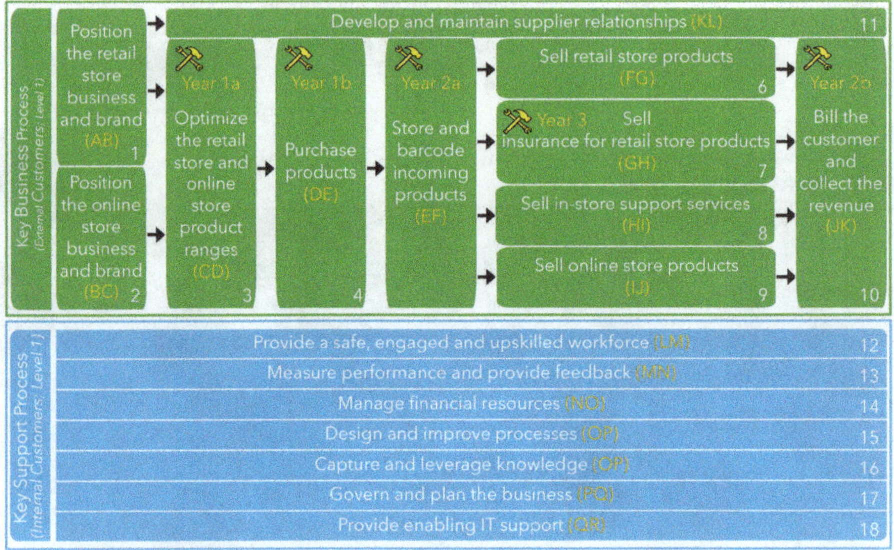

Indicative 1-page Process Model for an Aged Care Services Business

Our ROLE *(Level 0 process)*

We provide residential aged care services for the people of New South Wales.

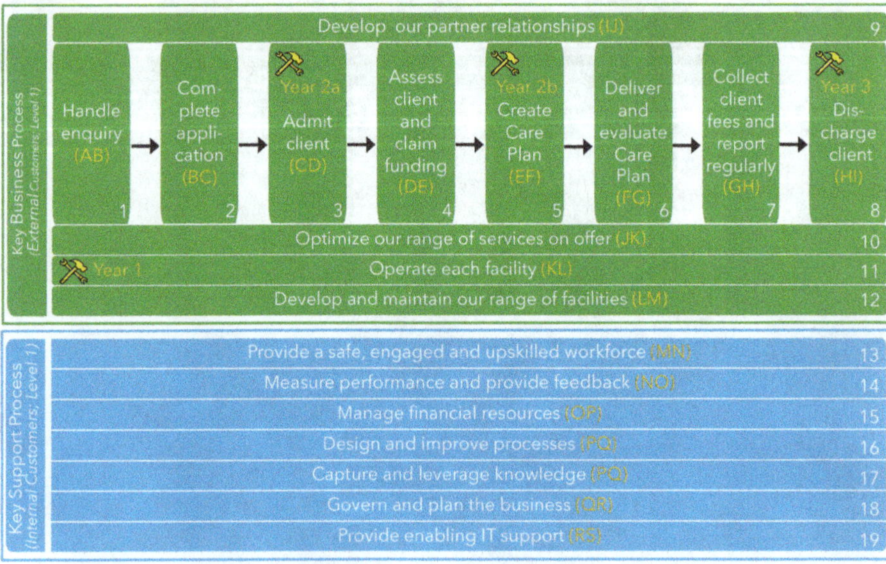

Indicative 1-page Process Model for an Energy Trading Business

Our ROLE *(Level 0 process)*

We develop, generate, trade and consult in renewable energy for Australia.

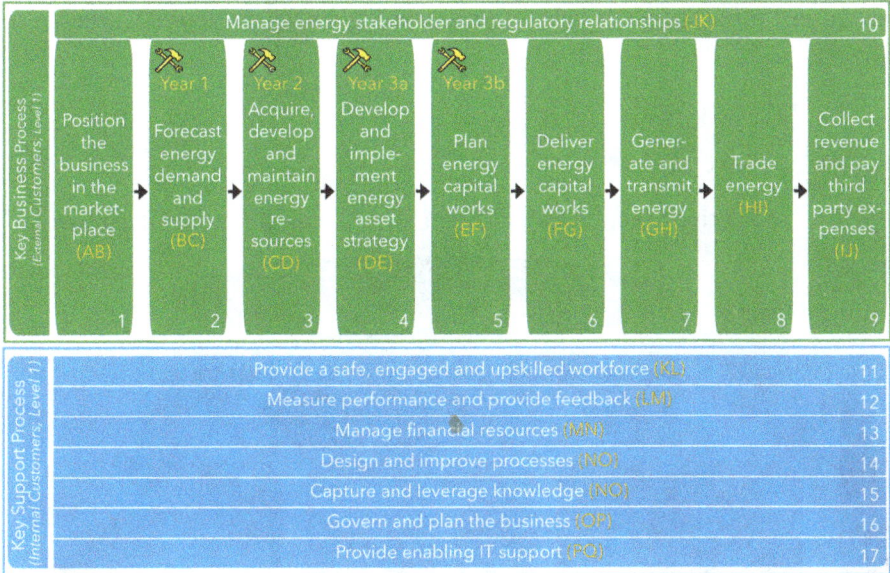

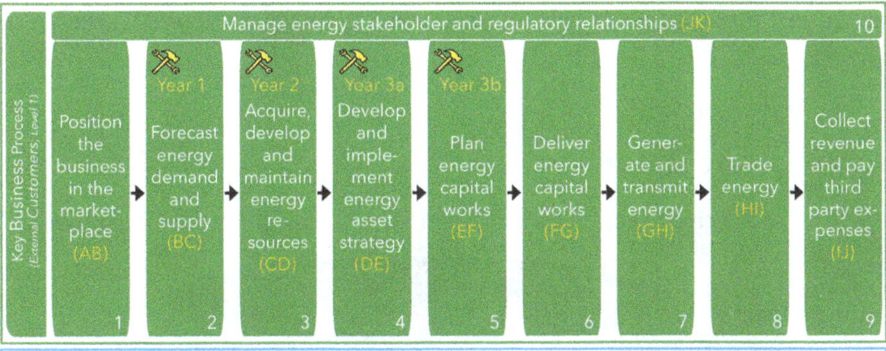

Key Support Process
(Internal Customers, Level 1)

- Provide a safe, engaged and upskilled workforce (KL) 11
- Measure performance and provide feedback (LM) 12
- Manage financial resources (MN) 13
- Design and improve processes (NO) 14
- Capture and leverage knowledge (NO) 15
- Govern and plan the business (OP) 16
- Provide enabling IT support (PQ) 17

APPENDIX C: Examples of 1-page Strategic Plans

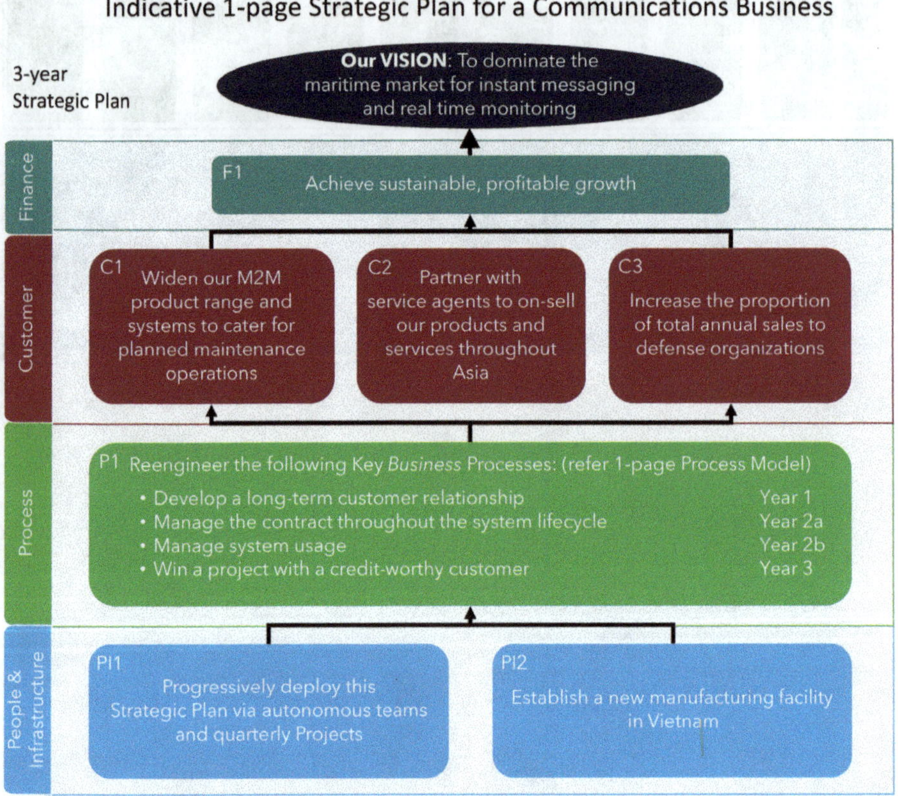

Indicative 1-page Strategic Plan for a Communications Business
3-year Strategic Plan
Our VISION: To dominate the maritime market for instant messaging and real time monitoring
Finance
F1 Achieve sustainable, profitable growth
Customer
C1 Widen our M2M product range and systems to cater for planned maintenance operations
C2 Partner with service agents to on-sell our products and services throughout Asia
C3 Increase the proportion of total annual sales to defense organizations
Process
P1 Reengineer the following Key Business Processes: (refer 1-page Process Model)
• Develop a long-term customer relationship Year 1
• Manage the contract throughout the system lifecycle Year 2a
• Manage system usage Year 2b
• Win a project with a credit-worthy customer Year 3
People & Infrastructure
PI1 Progressively deploy this Strategic Plan via autonomous teams and quarterly Projects
PI2 Establish a new manufacturing facility in Vietnam

Indicative 1-page Strategic Plan for a Luxury Travel Business

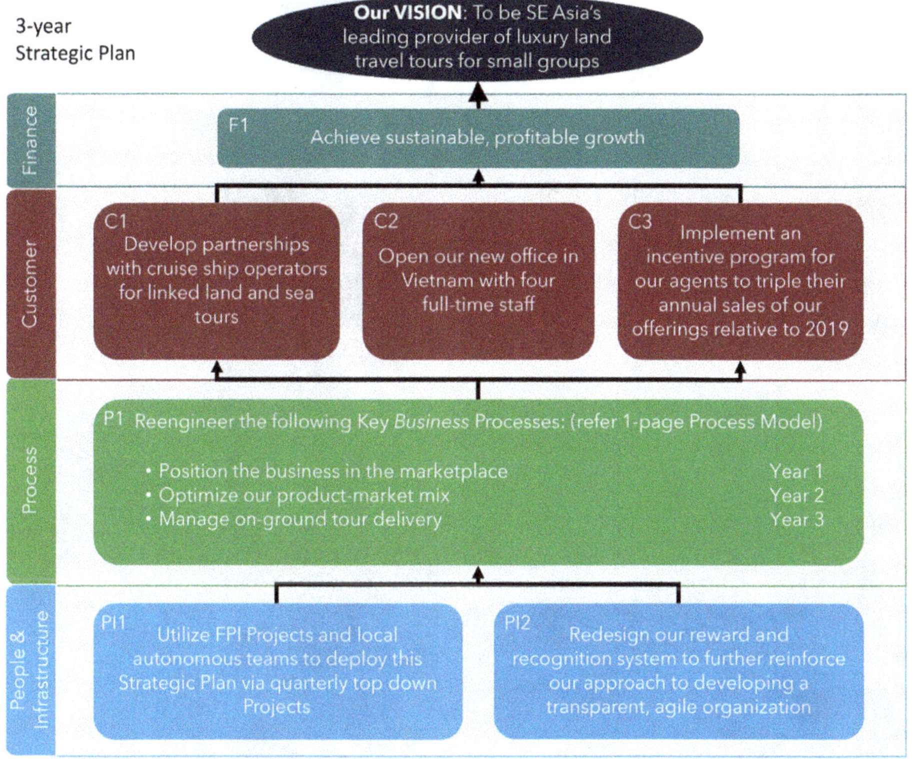
3-year
Strategic Plan
Our VISION: To be SE Asia's leading provider of luxury land travel tours for small groups
Finance
F1
Achieve sustainable, profitable growth
Customer
C1
Develop partnerships with cruise ship operators for linked land and sea tours
C2
Open our new office in Vietnam with four full-time staff
C3
Implement an incentive program for our agents to triple their annual sales of our offerings relative to 2019
Process
P1 Reengineer the following Key Business Processes: (refer 1-page Process Model)
• Position the business in the marketplace Year 1
• Optimize our product-market mix Year 2
• Manage on-ground tour delivery Year 3
People & Infrastructure
PI1
Utilize FPI Projects and local autonomous teams to deploy this Strategic Plan via quarterly top down Projects
PI2
Redesign our reward and recognition system to further reinforce our approach to developing a transparent, agile organization

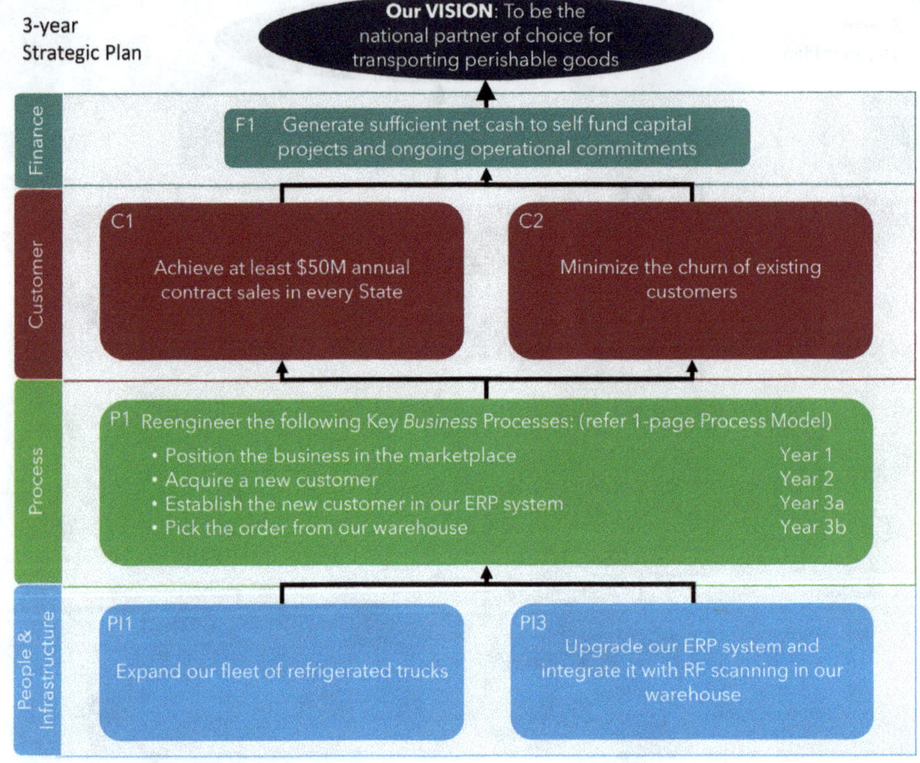
Indicative 1-page Strategic Plan for a Transport Business
3-year
Strategic Plan
Our VISION: To be the national partner of choice for transporting perishable goods
Finance
F1 Generate sufficient net cash to self fund capital projects and ongoing operational commitments
Customer
C1
Achieve at least $50M annual contract sales in every State
C2
Minimize the churn of existing customers
Process
P1 Reengineer the following Key Business Processes: (refer 1-page Process Model)
• Position the business in the marketplace Year 1
• Acquire a new customer Year 2
• Establish the new customer in our ERP system Year 3a
• Pick the order from our warehouse Year 3b
People & Infrastructure
PI1
Expand our fleet of refrigerated trucks
PI3
Upgrade our ERP system and integrate it with RF scanning in our warehouse

Indicative 1-page Strategic Plan for a Student Residential College

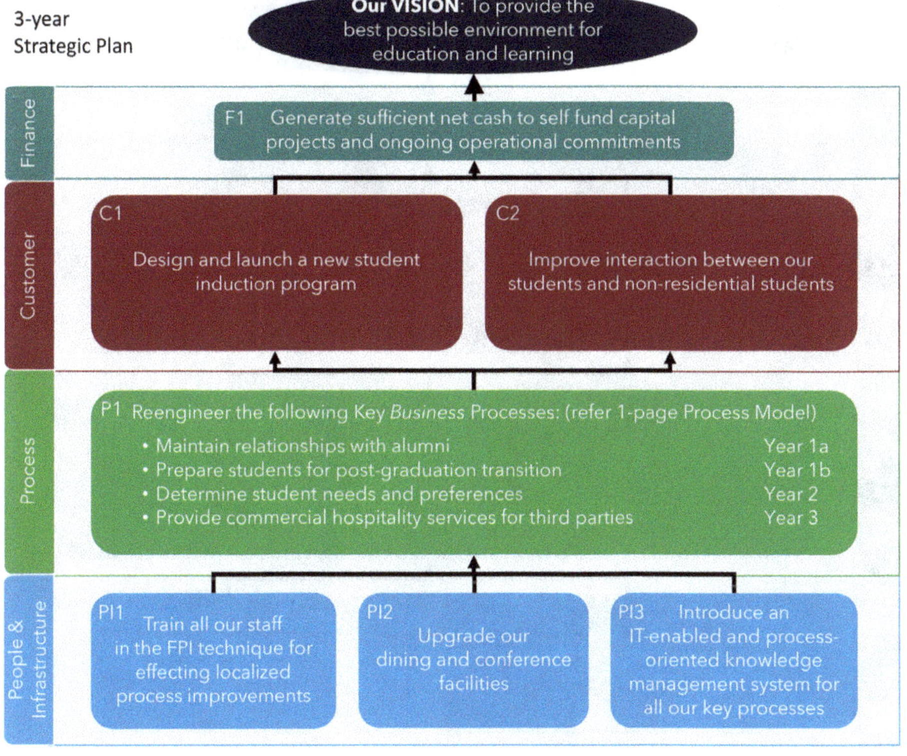
3-year
Strategic Plan
Our VISION: To provide the best possible environment for education and learning
Finance
F1 Generate sufficient net cash to self fund capital projects and ongoing operational commitments
Customer
C1
Design and launch a new student induction program
C2
Improve interaction between our students and non-residential students
Process
P1 Reengineer the following Key Business Processes: (refer 1-page Process Model)
• Maintain relationships with alumni Year 1a
• Prepare students for post-graduation transition Year 1b
• Determine student needs and preferences Year 2
• Provide commercial hospitality services for third parties Year 3
People & Infrastructure
PI1 Train all our staff in the FPI technique for effecting localized process improvements
PI2 Upgrade our dining and conference facilities
PI3 Introduce an IT-enabled and process-oriented knowledge management system for all our key processes

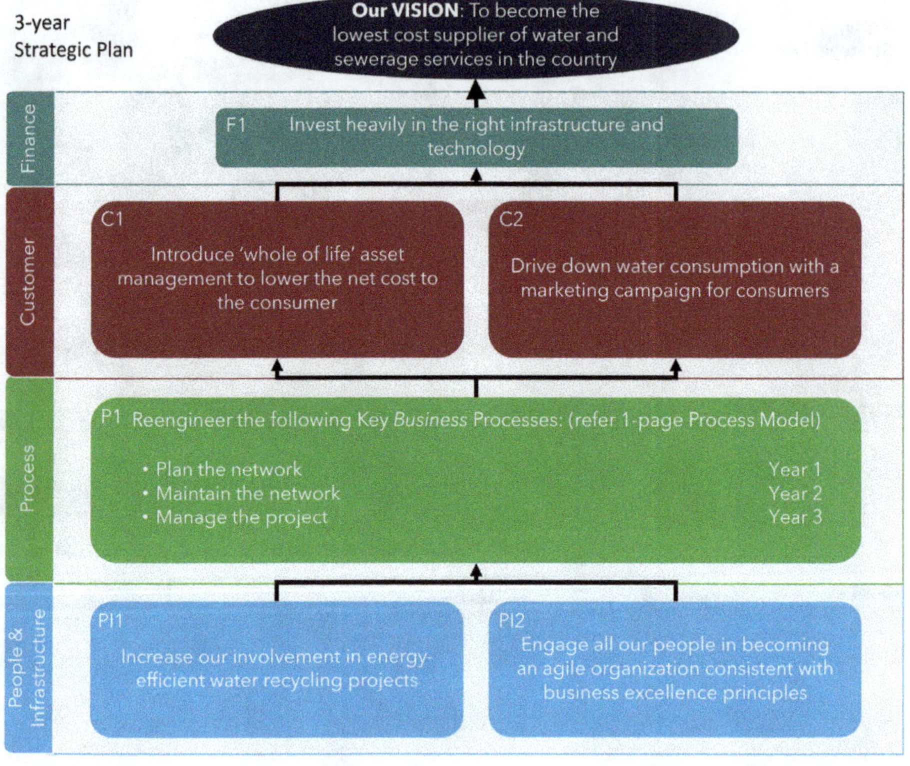
Indicative 1-page Strategic Plan for a Water and Sewerage Utility
3-year Strategic Plan
Our VISION: To become the lowest cost supplier of water and sewerage services in the country
Finance
F1 Invest heavily in the right infrastructure and technology
Customer
C1 Introduce 'whole of life' asset management to lower the net cost to the consumer
C2 Drive down water consumption with a marketing campaign for consumers
Process
P1 Reengineer the following Key Business Processes: (refer 1-page Process Model)
• Plan the network Year 1
• Maintain the network Year 2
• Manage the project Year 3
People & Infrastructure
PI1 Increase our involvement in energy-efficient water recycling projects
PI2 Engage all our people in becoming an agile organization consistent with business excellence principles

About the Authors

Dr Mark Rehn, BE PhD MBA FAICD FIEAUST CPEng FIMC CMC, Founder, My Business Excellence®

Dr Rehn's mission is to help SMEs implement best practices for running their businesses.

During the 1980s and 1990s, Dr Rehn was managing director of Aptech Australia, one of Australia's leading management consultancies. He led the teams that developed the federally funded methodologies for World Competitive Manufacturing (WCM) and for Total Quality Management (TQM) and introduced them into Australian and New Zealand businesses via several hundred specially trained consultancy firms. The firm's focus for these 14 years was on helping SME clients formulate and execute strategy through process improvement.

Aptech Australia was acquired by IBM Global Services in 1996. Over the next 5 years, Dr Rehn undertook leadership roles in Business Transformation, Strategic Partnering, and Knowledge Management for Australia, New Zealand and the Asia Pacific Region.

Working as an independent consultant since 2001, Dr Rehn has helped SMEs understand and implement business excellence. In collaboration with Mark James over the past 8 years, he has progressively converted his successful consulting methodology into the My Business Excellence® web-based offering designed exclusively for SMEs.

Throughout his consulting career, Dr Rehn has worked with more than 1,000 client organizations. He remains a prolific presenter for the international network of CEOs known as The Executive Connection (TEC) on the topic of how best to implement Business Excellence. He is also a regular speaker at the Leadership Thinktank and the CEO Network.

Mark James, BSc, CEO, My Business Excellence®

Mark has a passion for Business Transformation through the strategic implementation of technology. He spent his early professional years consulting on software technologies to Enterprises and SMEs in Australia, Europe and Asia. In 2010 he founded his business Smarta Systems, with a strong desire to improve business performance through better data-driven decision making. An initial focus on data analytics rapidly moved into data and process-driven software solutions. Mark is very comfortable straddling the line between business and technology and ensuring that the technology is working for the company.

As co-creator of My Business Excellence platform, Mark has collaborated with Mark Rehn over the last eight years to evolve Mark's original consulting methodology into a modern platform approach that is accessible across the globe. He has a strong desire to see businesses worldwide implement continuous improvement, develop the associated culture and reap substantial financial benefits as a result.

www.ingramcontent.com/pod-product-compliance
Lightning Source LLC
Chambersburg PA
CBHW071605210326
41597CB00019B/3406

* 9 7 8 0 6 4 8 7 3 6 9 1 2 *